TRUST, OBEY, LISTEN, REJOICE!

TRUST, OBEY, LISTEN, REJOICE!

LESSONS IN DEVELOPING A CLOSER WALK WITH GOD

Joe Herzberg

XULON PRESS

Xulon Press
2301 Lucien Way #415
Maitland, FL 32751
407.339.4217
www.xulonpress.com

Edited by Xulon Press.

Printed in the United States of America.

ISBN-13: 978-1-54563-851-4

DEDICATION

This compilation of writings is dedicated to my family and especially my mother, Audrey Barbara Herzberg, who gave me the gift of my faith, reminding me repeatedly to seek first the kingdom of God and His righteousness, knowing that all else would be provided!

SPECIAL DEDICATION

Mother Mary, our Blessed Virgin, has stood by me through the years, lovingly showing me the way to her Son, Jesus. Like a beacon, Our Lady has kept me from crashing upon the rocks in my spiritual voyage, with the love of her Son always there to comfort me and encourage me toward a better day in His kingdom!

"Stella Maris"
Our Lady, Star of the Sea

Beacon of light
Guiding us away from dangerous shoals
Our hope in life's storms
To take us to the safety of your Son's love

Bright star of night
Encouraging us to cast into the deep
To catch souls, to bring hearts to our Savior

Even when skies are dark and foreboding
Knowing you are always there, beyond the horizon
Directing us to do whatever He tells us

Our Lady, Star of the Sea, pray for us!

CONTENTS

Chapter 1.
TRUST

Chapter 2.
OBEY

Chapter 3.

LISTEN

Chapter 4.
REJOICE

ABOUT THE AUTHOR

A cradle Catholic Christian, Joe Herzberg has been a life-long student of his faith, which included three of his teen years at a Catholic seminary in Savannah, Georgia. Soon afterward, Joe's vocation was his family, and with wife Stephanie reared eight children, and are now gifted with thirteen grandchildren. Several years ago Joe began writing and publishing weekly spiritual reflections that draw upon his life experiences and wisdom. He has compiled these into this first book of reflections.

In 2017, Joe was received into the Holy Family Catholic Lay Carmelite Community in Marietta, GA as a Third Order Lay Carmelite.

INTRODUCTION

This book is based upon four simple truths, which together and in sequence set forth a pathway to holiness and salvation. *Trust, Obey, Listen, Rejoice* is challenging, but hopeful, in knowing that our adherence to the will of God, seeking to obey His commandments and listening for His guidance will surely lead to finding true peace and joy, thus giving us reason to rejoice! Having sustainable joy is just not possible, I would submit, unless total surrender to God's will and purpose in our lives happens first.

Over the past five years my own life experience and spiritual struggles in rearing eight children, while being the primary family breadwinner, has inspired and compelled me to write more than 150 spiritual reflections to bring practicality in our journey to finding lasting peace and joy. These brief lessons speak to the struggles of daily living, addressing setbacks due to our sinful nature, always calling on God's infinite mercy to get us back on our feet and giving us hope that all will be okay.

Being present in the moment and choosing to be happy are two core principles to staying hopeful in our spiritual walk. God exists in each moment of our lives, giving us direction and reassurance. We should make the most of what I call the majesty of the moment, unencumbered by past disappointments and tomorrow's worries. Having a childlike faith in God, we should choose to be happy, knowing our heavenly Father has our best interests at heart. The choice of happiness is like an acquired taste, as we practice each day to reject negativity, to give God praise despite our disappointments and to see life as a glass half full.

My first reflection, "Trust, Obey, Listen, Rejoice," is included here for reading and contemplation, going deeper into the theme of this book and helping open our hearts to the various reflections that follow. I have chosen around sixty reflections, which have been grouped in one of the four truths. This is intended to help give the reader a context for the reflections, thus enabling that some grace or blessing might be realized.

Reflection—"Trust, Obey, Listen, Rejoice"

Trust – We must trust in God always and have a faith like that of a child, meaning no matter what, we have an absolute and unquestionable belief that God will take care of us. Trust means subjugating our own designs and ambitions for our lives to God's divine plan for each of us. Letting go of control over our lives gives us genuine freedom and peace. Yes, God has a plan for every person; yet we also have to obey, listen and rejoice in order to achieve lasting peace and salvation.

Obey – As Christians, we are taught the Ten Commandments. If we choose not to follow these commandments and find ourselves in open rebellion with God, we cannot achieve lasting happiness and salvation in Christ.

Listen – Like the songwriter who receives the inspiration for a new song, we must be ready for the incoming revelations from God, through the Holy Spirit, who will guide us and give us the right ideas and responses to life's challenges. I tell others that often times, when we are totally still and quiet, God can speak to us. It's not an actual voice we hear, but messages are laid on our hearts and minds. So keep your antenna up all the time, be still and pray, "Lord, do with me as You will." Be open to receiving God's revelations and direction.

Rejoice – Yes, rejoice as God is always with us. Having given control of our lives back to God, striving to obey His commandments and learning to speak less and hear more from God's abundance of wisdom, we can have greater confidence in knowing our lives are in good order. We can anticipate that God has our best interests at heart, and He will guide us accordingly. It's going to be okay. It may not be what we want, but we'll be just fine!

Chapter 1

TRUST

The Power of Expectancy in Prayer

E aster Sunday commemorates Jesus breaking us free from the chains and bondage of sin, opening heaven and life eternal through His passion, death and resurrection. Beyond comfort, this reality of salvation should embolden us to do more to win souls to Christ and to spread the good news through our words and deeds. Of course, divine assistance is provided, as grace, to help us get through the rough spots on our journeys.

Prayer is also required to keep us grounded spiritually, to thwart Satan from tripping us up through pride, should we begin believing it's all about us. Satan is also the prince of doubt, keeping us guessing about our gifts from God and whether we're good enough to proclaim Christ crucified and resurrected. If I am to err, let it be on the side of having confidence and therefore being bold enough to ask for big things in prayer. Jesus told us to ask for what we needed in His name, and He would grant our requests so that the Father may be glorified in the Son. Sure, it's the will of God that will prevail, but maybe we're too timid in asking for what we need to fulfill His purpose for us in living good and holy lives.

Saint Teresa of Calcutta, known as Mother Teresa, seemed to get the "ask whatever in Jesus' name," having boundless faith and expecting big things from Jesus in her zeal to serve the poorest of the poor. I once read that Mother Teresa wished to rescue thirty-six children caught in the crossfire in Beirut, Lebanon, as Israelis bombed enemy targets in 1982. She was advised by the diplomats that rescue was impossible. Not to be discouraged, Teresa, in a matter of fact way, told the diplomats that she was in prayer and she was certain there would be a cease fire to occur the following day, through the intercession of the Blessed Virgin Mary, in the name of Jesus, that would enable the rescue. To the astonishment of her naysayers, a cease fire soon happened, and rescue was accomplished. Mother Teresa was the ultimate prayer warrior.

So, on this day of resurrection and freedom from the bonds of sin, let's proceed with boldness and confidence in the power of our prayer, having trust and even an expectancy that God will do great things through us in our lives, if we will just let Him. We don't have to wait until Pentecost to implore the Holy Spirit to fire up our passions for good in proclaiming Christ's message of hope of eternal life, not just to our friends and family, but to the whole world!

We adore You, O Christ, and we praise You, because by Your holy cross, death and resurrection You have redeemed the world!

The Value of Redemptive Suffering

> "My grace is sufficient for you, for my power is made perfect in weakness. Therefore I will boast all the more gladly about my weaknesses, so that Christ's power may rest on me. That is why, for Christ's sake, I delight in weaknesses, in insults, in hardships, in persecutions, in difficulties. For when I am weak, then I am strong" (2 Corinthians 12:9-10).

Redemptive suffering conceptually might sound complicated, but the reality is simple. God has a way of allowing havoc to enter into our lives, not to punish us, but to remind us of our limitations and frailties, underscoring our utter reliance on His love, grace and mercy. For believers, an unexpected crisis or setback with our health, circumstances at home or at work, can serve to reset priorities, helping gain a healthy dose of humility, replacing more of our self-reliance with Christ-centeredness.

Consider enduring difficulties, such as any kind of sustained deprivation, loneliness, illness, spiritual dryness, feelings of being unwanted, even leanings toward despair, as means of purification. Rather than drifting off toward utter desolation and hopelessness, we should offer up to God our sorrows as a means of achieving spiritual cleansing, washing away any pretense of self-sufficiency, thereby drawing us even closer to the suffering Christ and preparing us for life everlasting in heaven. Knowing that our salvation is certain through the enduring love of God should help sustain us during difficult times.

Catholics believe purgatory is the means of purifying a believer, saved by the redemptive suffering of Jesus at Calvary, and being burnished, removing the impurities of the taint and consequences of our sinfulness, and allowing us to shine even more brightly as we enter the kingdom of heaven.

The apostle Paul experienced redemptive suffering through his often cited "thorn in the flesh." Three times he asked God to remove the "thorn," which was a reminder to Paul that, despite his many gifts, he lacked the mastery to conquer this personal fault, but for the will of God. Through grace, Paul came to understand that the nagging discomfort of an unconquerable flaw could be transcendent, as Jesus said, "My grace is sufficient," in dealing with his shortcomings.

Coming to terms with weakness went beyond providing a context for suffering, becoming transformative to Paul, as he wrote, "When I am weak, I am strong." We can unite our sufferings with those of a crucified Christ only by acknowledging that in weakness God's will and purpose can be made more clearly manifest and perfected. If spiritual growth depends on adversity, then Paul essentially said, "Bring it on." He concluded it was better to boast about his weaknesses, knowing God's best for him would more likely arise out of his brokenness than by way of his human strengths (see 2 Corinthians 12:5-10).

So think of hardships as God's way of refining us, more perfectly conforming our will and actions to His divine plan, enabling us to realize our purpose in this world more completely and preparing for the heavenly world to come.

> "Today, if you hear his voice, do not harden your hearts" (Hebrews 3:15).

"I Thirst"

As we recall this day the passion of Christ, at one moment during His slow, agonizing death on the cross Jesus spoke, asking for something to wet His parched, dry mouth. The guards taunted Him by putting a sponge soaked in vinegar on a long rod or stick and pushing the sponge to His mouth as one more act of degradation toward our Savior.

The words of Jesus, "I thirst", speak to the human need of hydration. Water symbolizes so much more, giving and sustaining life, and washing away our impurities. Jesus reminded the Samaritan woman at the well that His "living water" would not have to be replenished. Water represents sustenance in this life and the substance that brings life everlasting in heaven.

To Mother Teresa, "I thirst" was at the core of the mission of her Missionaries of Charity. Her life's work of giving comfort, beginning with the discarded and dying on the streets and in the gutters of Calcutta, answered a call that Jesus had a "thirst" for souls to be given dignity and love, even when filthy and disease-ridden. Teresa understood the maxim of Jesus that whatever was done for the least of His people was done to Him.

As we ponder the sufferings of Jesus, knowing He must die then rise from the dead to free the way for our salvation, remember that Jesus thirsts for our souls to be saved too. As Christ loves us uniquely and individually, He longs for each of us to put aside our cares and distractions then pick up our crosses to follow Him. The roadway to living a good and holy life is narrow indeed but guaranteed to bring us sustainable peace and happiness.

Jesus, we truly regret that our sins required You to experience torment and abuse by Your executioners. Through our pondering and recalling Your passion, may You touch our hearts with sorrow for our sins and spark resolve to turn around our lives for You. As the good thief asked You to remember him when You entered into Your kingdom, give me grace through Your ever-flowing spring of love so I might hear, upon my death, "Today you shall be with Me in paradise!"

Prayer from "The Way of the Cross" by Saint Alphonsus Liguori:

> "Never permit me to offend You again. Grant that I may love You always; and then do with me what You will."

"I Fall Down; I Get Up"

> "Then Peter came to Jesus and asked, 'Lord,
> how many times shall I forgive my brother and
> sister who sins against me? Up to seven times?'
> Jesus answered, 'I tell you, not seven times, but
> seventy-times seven'" (Matthew 18:21-22).

The lead up to the celebration of the birth of Jesus is a time for reflection, repentance and amending our lives so we can approach the new year with a fresh resolve to follow more closely God's will and purpose for our lives. Achieving a closer alignment is great, applying the principles of last Sunday's reflection, which was "Trust, Obey, Listen, Rejoice." Maintaining an adherence to a more straight and narrow life of virtue is the bigger challenge, with many of us lapsing into old sinful habits then having to come back to Jesus, contrite, asking forgiveness and absolution and promising to amend our lives. "Lord, this time I mean it," we might pray.

There is something about knowing better, yet falling short anyway, that can cause us to question God's willingness to pick us up again and again, delivering us from our failings, despite Jesus telling Peter that His mercy is boundless. The mercy we are called to extend to our neighbor is a reflection of God's willingness to forgive us too.

Placing such high expectations on ourselves, we might, in despair, give up or check out for a while. Thinking our spiritual ambitions are unattainable, we might replace God's way with our own devices, destined to leave us lacking and potentially threatening our salvation and life eternal in heaven.

The apostle Paul gives us some context around the inevitability of human frailty and God's power finding perfection in our weaknesses. In 2 Corinthians 12, Paul begged God to remove the "thorn in his flesh," which was some nagging problem or shortcoming that plagued him. In response, God replied, "My grace is sufficient for you, for my power is made perfect in weakness." And Paul replied, with an apparent sigh of relief, "Therefore I will boast all the more gladly about my weaknesses, so that Christ's power may rest on me. That is why, for Christ's sake, I delight in my weakness, in insults, in hardships, in persecutions, in difficulties. For when I am weak, then I am strong" (2 Corinthians 12: 9-10).

Even the cloistered monastics have their failings. As I recall, a Trappist monk once remarked that his life of communing with God in a very special way in prayer, works and solitude was a repetition of "I fall down; I get up." I guess our saints experienced much the same thing. It's our human condition, although the key words of "getting up" and then "staying up" become a differentiator.

God didn't put us on this earth to be scrupulous and miserable, but to live an abundant life, receiving many blessings. Seeking perfection may seem admirable, but it is frankly unrealistic and maddening. Making a concerted effort, seeking God's grace, to amend our lives is reasonable enough. Just don't stay down too long when you fall. Believe the love of Jesus is infinite and His capacity to forgive us is unlimited, with no limit to His mercy. When we fail, go quickly to confess and seek absolution from God. We cannot outstrip His willingness to forgive us and through grace to help us avoid falling again.

Father, as we will soon celebrate the birth of Your gift to us, Your Son, Jesus, may we find time to be still, to reflect on the glory of the Savior of the world, born in a stable but destined to save us from destruction. May we remember the words of Jesus that we seek first Your kingdom and Your righteousness and that all we need will be added, including the capacity to get up again and again when we fall down.

Guess Who's Coming to Dinner?—Thoughts on Jesus and Zacchaeus

"Jesus entered Jericho and was passing through. A man was there by the name of Zacchaeus; he was a chief tax collector and was wealthy. He wanted to see who Jesus was, but because he was short he could not see over the crowd. So he ran ahead and climbed a sycamore-fig tree since Jesus was coming that way.

"When Jesus reached the spot, he looked up and said to him, 'Zacchaeus, come down immediately. I must stay at your house today.' So he came down at once and welcomed him gladly" (Luke 19:1-6).

As I am listening to today's Gospel reading, I wondered what I would do if Jesus informed me He was coming to stay at my house. This is nuts as I am going through the paces mentally of calling my wife and asking that we get all ready for our special guest, adding that we would have much work to do to make-sure we gave a positive impression. The visit would probably be brief; so let's get it right, and we can relax some after He departs. It's all about first impressions, right?

Of course, hurried, last-minute preparations will likely fall short in preparing for the coming of the Lord. Jesus knew Zacchaeus was ready. This outcast tax collector, who made his fortune by extorting money from those less fortunate and being short in stature, climbed a tree so he could see Jesus in the crowd. I suspect that Zacchaeus wanted redemption and that Jesus sensed his wanting to be converted and therefore chose to stay at his home. The response to give half of what he owned to the poor and make extra amends with those he victimized signified a sincere desire on the part of Zacchaeus to change his life. Jesus then proclaimed, "Today salvation has come to this house, because this man, too, is a son of Abraham. For the Son of Man came to seek and to save the lost" (Luke 19:9-10). Jesus could always see beyond the super-ficial and could read hearts, knowing one's sincerity.

So back to the visit to my home during my musings at today's Mass. What would Jesus think about my heart? I could rattle off things in my life that show a sincere desire to trust in God, obey His commandments and be open to His direction. But I expect Jesus would go to the inner recesses of my heart to call out the incongruities, the gaps between talk and action, a lack of charity and my somewhat tepid response, at times, to His call to seek first His kingdom in all I do. As much as I might believe my salvation is well within my grasp, my special hypothetical dinner guest may shake me up a bit. He may remind me that the path to life everlasting is narrow and that I must rid myself of anything that would distract me, especially pride when I think "I got this." Love of God and neighbor must be evident as well as a sincere desire to seek God's will and purpose in all I do.

Unlike Zacchaeus, we as Christians should know better and not have a bunch of excuses at the ready to justify our falling short of the mark with God. It's not about perfection because we all have a history of falling then getting back up. Instead, this is about humility, knowing we just can't do this journey without the love of Jesus.

Are you ready for Jesus to stay at your home?

> "Today, if you would hear His voice, Do not harden your hearts" (Psalm 95: 7-8).

St. Therese of Lisieux—Her Vocation is Love

In our prayer life, is there a point where we might hesitate in asking God for help, thinking our need is so small or even a bit trivial that it doesn't deserve the attention of an almighty God? We are told "not to sweat the small stuff"; yet the little annoyances of life, left unchecked, can put some distance in our feelings from the love of our Savior. In contrast, consider that minor trials and disappointments present an opportunity to bear up quietly, in essence making a small sacrifice as an act of love for Jesus, knowing that Jesus as the Son of Man bore extreme pain for our sins at Calvary.

This rather mystical approach to turning life's minor challenges into a sign of love for Jesus was at the heart of the brief ministry of a cloistered Carmelite nun, Therese Martin. Born in France in 1873 to devout Catholic parents, Louis and Zelie, Therese was the youngest of nine children, her father's "Little Queen." When only four years old, little Therese experienced the devastation of the loss of her mother, who had herself witnessed the early death of several of her young children. Therese became emotionally and physically frail, and during one of her bouts of illness her spirits were lifted when she reported seeing the Blessed Virgin smiling at her through the statue of Mary near her sick bed. She quickly recovered, and this experience became a revelation, helping lead Therese to seek a life of service of love for Jesus.

For Therese, this calling would find fruition through life as a Carmelite nun. She longed to join the Carmel monastery at Lisieux, where two of her sisters had already joined. The problem was that Therese was but fourteen years old, and she was unable to persuade her bishop that she was ready to pursue her passion. Around that time, her father, Louis, took Therese along on a Vatican pilgrimage. There, during an audience with Pope Leo XIII, Therese implored the Holy Father to grant her permission to join the Carmel. Pope Leo said such a decision was solely dependent on God's will; yet Therese persisted unsuccessfully, ultimately having to be taken from the reception room by Vatican guards.

Not to be denied, Therese was soon granted permission at age fifteen to enter the Carmel monastery at Lisieux. Imbued by the wisdom of the Holy Spirit, Therese understood the beauty and majesty of seemingly small or unimportant things in our lives. She remarked about God's favor as much for the little flowers in a garden as the larger, more impressive orchids and so forth. Even in those things less significant, God's love is made manifest, including those small sacrifices.

Although she desired to serve God in many ways and different places, Therese never left her community, living a simple existence in her Carmel at Lisieux. Her life was cut short by tuberculosis, and at just twenty-four she passed away, almost unnoticed outside of Lisieux. Before she died, Therese wrote about her experiences and spiritual conversion, which was posthumously published as her autobiography, *The Story of a Soul*.

News of the "Little Flower" spread rapidly, and Therese, in death, became an inspiration, helping save souls throughout the world for Jesus. Therese had foretold her future in heaven when she wrote: "I will spend my heaven doing good on earth." Therese was made a saint by Pope Pius XI in 1925 and declared a Doctor of the Church by St. John Paul II in 1997, which was amazing testament to the profound impact of her seemingly simple life in Lisieux.

St. Therese, our "Little Flower," may do some good for our lives, helping us to see beauty in the small, trivial and insignificant of this world, including small sacrifices, where God's love is made manifest in a sweet and special way. St. Therese, send us some flowers from heaven, so we too may lead with love, nudging others along to find lasting peace and joy in knowing the love, mercy and redemption found in Jesus.

Jesus, talk to me, talk to my spirit,
Jesus, speak to me, speak to my heart!

Mother Angelica—Rekindling a Love of My Catholic Faith

"And He said to them, 'Go into all the world and preach the good news to all creation'" (Mark 16:15).

I recall listening to Mother Angelica, founder of the Eternal Word Television Network (EWTN), on an AM radio while vacationing at the Georgia coast back in the 1990s. Her shows were broadcast from an affiliated Catholic radio station in Jacksonville Beach. Around that time I had also been listening to Christian evangelists on the radio and was particularly fond of Bishop T. D. Jakes, whose "get ready, get ready, get ready" preaching fired me up in pursuit of a deeper level of personal spirituality.

14

For me, Mother Angelica was a Catholic evangelist who also stimulated my faith, not so much by her keen intellect or emotionally charged preaching, but by her speaking to my heart. She pulled me in through her homespun, down-to-earth lessons, telling stories laced with humor and always adding some truth about my Catholic faith. She was uncompromising in stressing the importance of the real presence of the Eucharist as the body, blood, soul and divinity of Jesus. Going to confession became a theme on her programs, with her reminding us that we risked losing our immortal souls by neglecting to ask God for forgiveness through the Sacrament of Penance.

When I reflect on Mother Angelica's influence, I realize she had taken me back to my Catholic upbringing, largely influenced by the Sisters of Mercy at Sacred Heart School in Augusta, Georgia, many years ago. I came up in the days of the Baltimore Catechism, where right and wrong seemed to be more clearly understood. Orthodoxy around Catholic teachings was the order of the day, and I was to live my life accordingly. Attending Mass each Sunday, along with Holy Days of Obligation, Forty Hours of Devotion and so on, not to mention lining up on Saturdays for confession at my parish church, was routine.

Like so many Catholics, I had remained faithful but became distracted and broke away some from the spiritual moorings of my youth. I got sloppy with my faith and became totally absorbed with being a husband and father and making a living. So meeting Mother Angelica through radio and cable television gradually pulled me back to my authentic Catholic roots. I might say that she helped save my soul.

The inheritance of our Catholic faith is a call to reflect the love of Jesus in our lives, for the sake of our souls. Mother Angelica reminds us that our love of Jesus must also serve to bring others to knowing Him, understanding that peace, joy and life everlasting in heaven have been made possible through our Lord's suffering, death and resurrection.

Mother Angelica often reminded us that we are called to be great saints and that we must be mindful not to miss this opportunity. Having a constancy in our faith, being uncompromising in calling out sin and seeking God's kingdom first in all we do take us down the path to holiness. Most important, all we do must be wrapped in an abounding love of God and our neighbor.

Mother Angelica would say to us today, "Let's get busy!"

St. Teresa of Avila—Doing Whatever Love Stirred Her to Do

> "After He (Jesus) had finished speaking, He said to Simon, 'Put out into deep water and lower your nets for a catch.' Simon said in reply, 'Master, we have worked hard all night and have caught nothing, but at your command I will lower the nets.' When they had done this, they caught a great number of fish and their nets were tearing" (Luke 5:4-6). (NAB – Revised Edition)

"His mother said to the servers, 'Do whatever
He tells you'" (John 2:5). (NAB - Revised Edition)

I once heard a Trappist monk explain (on a video about Mepkin Abbey near Charleston, South Carolina) that we need to go deeper than a surface-level understanding of God's love for us in our lives. The challenge for most of us is that it's hard to get beyond the noise and urgency of our preoccupation with our daily to-do lists, including worrying about our families, jobs and so forth. In Luke 5, Jesus tells Simon to strike out into the deep, to go beyond his worries and self-imposed limitations about what amazing things and "catches" God can make possible in his life. His mother would instruct us as she did the servants at the wedding feast at Cana, "Do whatever He tells you."

For the believer who wants to go deeper, St. Teresa of Avila's life and writings will show the way. Teresa was born in Avila, Spain, in 1515. As a young girl, Teresa possessed a charming manner and personality, making lots of friends who were complimentary of her. Despite her popularity, Teresa wasn't so pleased with herself, thinking she was a miserable sinner. Concerned with her welfare, her father thought it best to send her to a convent school. It was there she discovered her calling to a religious life as a Carmelite nun. Against her father's wishes she entered the Carmel of the Incarnation at Avila in 1535.

It would take twenty more years before Teresa experienced a spiritual conversion, going beyond a surface-level understanding of God's plan for her life. Life in the convent was very different at that time, as an abundance of material wealth could influence a decision to permit entry as might one's spiritual depth and intention. Against this more casual and less rigorous backdrop, Teresa was inspired to reform the convents to bring a return to greater levels of prayer, contemplation and self-denial. What followed was immense activity as she went about founding seventeen reformed Carmelite convents and two monasteries, more devoted to a life focused on prayer, contemplation and simplicity.

Teresa became a prolific writer, with her *Interior Castle* setting forth a pathway to deeper spirituality and closeness with God. She wrote about meeting God on the interior of our being, where exists a wellspring in which the flowing waters of God's love bring a greater sense of His presence in our lives. Here also we are taunted and tempted by Satan, who is even more determined to deny us that peace and joy made possible through joining our hopes and dreams with God's will and purpose.

We are reminded not to despair, but to do what God's love instructs us to do each day. Teresa reassures us that, despite our fears, God's love is sufficient. She writes: "Let nothing disturb you. Let nothing frighten you. All things are passing away: God never changes. Patience obtains all things. Whoever has God lacks nothing; God alone suffices." (Poem by St. Teresa of Avila)

Why Prayer Matters

> "'While it is true that I neither fear God nor respect any human being, because this widow

keeps bothering me I shall deliver a just decision for her lest she finally come and strike me.' The Lord said, "Pay attention to what the dishonest judge says. Will not God then secure the rights of His chosen ones who call out to Him day and night? Will He be slow to answer them? I tell you, He will see to it that justice is done for them speedily" (Luke 18: 4-8). (NAB - Revised Edition)

For me, prayer has always been a challenge. I guess for too long my approach to prayer had been one of needing to pray for fear of what would happen if I didn't. This "fear of God" attitude respected the belief that I was dependent on God for my family, my work, my health and so on. Yet the fear part had more to do with my own unresolved sin and unsteadiness spiritually, hoping God would help me anyway. When I heard about undeserved grace, this perhaps was an acknowledgment that God would help me and I could make an effort to clean up my act later. Really?

In the reading from Luke about the determined widow who petitioned the unjust judge to deal with her enemy, Jesus assured us that if the unjust judge provided relief for the widow who was "pestering" him, certainly God the Father would respond to the petitions of His elect and speedily. Taking Christ at His word, prayer does matter. I believe it's our faith, though, that God will provide for our needs that is key and not that we throw up lots of petitions when we're in crisis, hoping some will stick and a benevolent God will get us out of a jam.

So does quality matter in prayer? Of course, God can and will respond to prayer, irrespective of motives, the worthiness of the petitioner or the manner in which prayers are offered. For me, quality matters only because prayer should be an integral part of my spirituality, my daily walk with Jesus.

More mature prayer should be a reflection of a genuine effort to conform our lives to God's will and purpose, knowing we will fall short, guaranteed. We come back again and again, confessing our sins, being cleansed of the heaviness of our failings through God's grace and then starting over again. By taking up our crosses each day and petitioning God for our needs, in and out of crisis, we have greater confidence God is with us and will bless us. Prayer is an acknowledgment that God is integral to all we do each day.

Jesus, talk to me, talk to my spirit;
Jesus, speak to me, speak to my heart!

All of a Sudden, Life Happens!

"Therefore keep watch, because you do not know on what day your Lord will come.... So you also must be ready, because the Son of Man will come at an hour when you do not expect Him" (Matthew 24:42, 44).

It's very easy to get so caught up in our daily routines, almost unknowingly developing an expectation that the next day or next week will be just like the last. The thought that something tragic could radically change our realities, upending the reliability and comfort of the rhythm of life seems to belong to someone else, the next guy, but certainly not to us. Closer to home, we recently had a harsh reminder that life does happen. A serious car accident critically injured two of our family. As my brother-in-law clings to life on a ventilator and my sister-in-law faces challenging health complications from the accident, we are reminded of our fragility, our lack of control of things and our utter dependence on God.

Our grasp of our faith in God may provide some sense of protection against the unforeseen. But the potential for losing a loved one due to some accident or other freakish event may shatter our trust in God as we ask why a good God would allow something terrible to happen. Trying to analyze the "why" in human terms often comes up short. When we distance ourselves from our spirituality, however, we are left to our own devices and end up even more frustrated.

In the New Testament, when Jesus asked Peter if he would leave Him, Peter responded, "Lord, to whom shall we go? You have the words of eternal life" (see John 6:68). Peter understood, through the wisdom given him by the Holy Spirit, that he had nothing to sustain him like the love of Jesus. As we grow in our Christian faith, we can profess Christ crucified and resurrected as our source of strength, yet keep trying to do things our way, as if it is up to us to figure it out.

If we want to experience a sustainable level of peace and confidence, even in the midst of tragedy, we have to surrender our lives to God's will and purpose completely and unconditionally. This means applying the principle Jesus gave us that we seek first the kingdom of God and His righteousness, and all we need will be provided (see Matthew 6:33).

Instead of fretting each day over what might happen to us, we must replace our worry and self-dependence with daily prayer and devotions, asking God for guidance and protection, saying to Him, "Lord, do with me as You will."

Father, bless my family during this difficult time and allow healing to our injured loved ones. Use this crisis as an opportunity to bring our family closer and warm our hearts to the love of Your Son, Jesus, to comfort and sustain us. May we have the faith of a child, as Jesus taught us, believing without condition that God allows all things to happen for the good of our souls, amen!

In closing, here are four faith pillars to consider each day: Trust, Obey, Listen and Rejoice. Having an unquestioning trust in God, obeying His commandments and listening daily for God's direction, we can rejoice in knowing that things may not always turn out to our liking, but we will be just fine!

Finding Ourselves in a Dark Place

"Amen, amen, I say to you, unless a grain of
wheat falls in the ground and dies, it remains

> just a grain of wheat; but if it dies, it produces much fruit. Whoever loves his life loses it, and whoever hates his life in this world will preserve it for eternal life" (John 12:24-25). (NAB – Revised Edition)

Among the many television evangelists, I have been particularly inspired by Bishop T. D. Jakes of the Potter's House in Dallas, Texas. Jakes has a knack for taking the gospel message of hope and salvation and connecting to our daily realities, our human frailties and our desire to find lasting peace and joy. He recently preached a message on the hidden potential in a simple apple seed and how we must endure the dark places of life for God to prepare us for greater things.

Using our finite intellectual capacity, it's hard to fathom how a seed can grow and bear fruit, much less spawn an orchard of trees. As we were taught as kids, an apple seed cannot realize its potential until buried in soil and put "in a dark place." Through the process of germination and thereby creating new life, the seed will die away. The orchard can never be realized until the apple seed is put in the ground, in the darkness of the soil.

We too may find ourselves in dark places in our lives, due to loss, disappointments, setbacks in our health, our employment, our marriages and so forth. When we lose some of our sense of security, esteem or purpose, darkness will likely follow. Rather than questioning the circumstances or saying, "Woe is me," consider that a metamorphosis may be in the works. The

Father may allow us to experience times of doubt and sorrow in order to draw us closer to His Son, Jesus, to more completely realize His divine will, purpose and mission for each of us. Like the apple seed, perhaps some changes will be required in our lives, such as dying to our proclivities to sin and detaching ourselves from disordered cares and affections, or maybe just to rest a bit in order for us to bear new fruit and do even greater things for God's kingdom.

As we grow less dependent on anything but the love of Christ, our spirituality may morph into a greater level of intimacy with the crucified Christ, where, as St. Paul wrote, "It's not I who lives, but Christ who lives in me" (see Galatians 2:20). This spiritual change, or "metanoia" (from the Greek for "changing one's mind," meaning a transformation) brings us into a closer communion with Jesus, where we see His hand more often in matters large and small.

Using a different metaphor, Jesus, as the keeper of our spiritual vineyard, prunes us periodically to cut away some of our dead branches, allowing new life to grow, with the resulting fruit tasting even sweeter than before. The lesson of this reflection is that we should not be unduly fearful of experiencing setbacks, disappointments or losses. We know as Christians that God will often permit us to be shaken up and taken down a few pegs for the good of our souls, to purge us of our notions of self-sufficiency, to prune away the junk in our lives and to more keenly burnish our witness, preparing us for new and invigorating challenges and blessings in our future.

Coming out of the dark places, may the light of Christ shine more brightly in our words, actions and witness, invigorating us to do even greater things for the kingdom, through Jesus' name, we pray, amen.

Trying to Find Peace in the Midst of a Storm

Okay, I have been put to the test. Having experienced two ice and snow emergencies in Georgia in just three weeks was challenging enough. During the first event I fell on the ice and bruised or cracked at least one rib walking to my car. Thinking I could be home in about thirty minutes, I left work but never made it home. Instead I found myself stranded after three hours, unable to move on an icy road. It was 11:30 at night, and I had to leave my car and trudge, my side hurting, through the ice to a nearby hotel. Huddled in the hotel lobby with other weather "refugees," I was able to secure a room around 1:30 a.m. Two days later I made it home.

The second ice-and-snow event went much better. I stayed off the roads and waited it out for a day and a half, avoiding the icy conditions. My ribs were still sore but doing better. I returned to work, and everything seemed all right, except the weather reports from Augusta were concerning. The Weather Channel had a correspondent in Augusta, due to an expectation of heavy ice formation on trees and power lines.

Being a commuter working in the Atlanta area with my family and home in Augusta, the news from home began sounding ominous. Beginning Wednesday night, reports of power outages from broken tree limbs falling on power lines came in from my seven of my eight sons and daughters, who all live in the Augusta area. All reported power was out, and no one had heat. Thursday evening was a repeat: no power, no heat.

I arrived in Augusta late afternoon Friday to find massive damage due to hundreds of fallen or broken trees. It looked like the aftermath of a tornado or hurricane. The situation at my home was the same, with one large tree that had fallen, but no damage to the house. When darkness fell, we prepared to sleep in the house, with hopes that our power would be restored soon. It was around 10:30 p.m. on Friday when I pulled extra covers over me so I could sleep in our dark, cold home. Meanwhile, my wife, Stephanie, sat in her car, charging her phone.

Just when I thought I could get some rest I felt the bed begin to vibrate, then the house. It sounded as if a helicopter might be trying to land nearby. I knew that was unlikely and realized the rattling noise must have been an earthquake. My next thought was God wanted to get our attention for some reason and began to ponder what might come next.

The good news: Power was restored Saturday afternoon, and as of Monday, only my son Joey and his family remained without power in their North Augusta home. We had a couple of aftershocks from the Friday earthquake; yet it appeared that life may be back to normal, maybe.

Father, I am reminded that "Trust, Obey, Listen and Rejoice" applies even in the midst of the storms we face. When facing a crisis, bolster our faith and give us extra graces to make us stronger so we can give You the glory, knowing everything You allow to happen in our lives is for the good of our souls. We ask these things in the name of Your Son, Jesus, amen.

Chapter 2

OBEY

Pulling Sinfulness Out by the Root

Having confessed our sins and being determined to sin no more, why do we have setbacks? Is our devotion to Jesus lacking in some way that we fall back on old habits?

I once read about the Trappist monk who described his life as a repetition of "I fall, then I get up." I have also heard a Christian preacher say that as we achieve a closer walk with Christ, relapses remind us of how much we need Jesus' love and grace to sustain us on our path to greater holiness.

For me, there comes a point when it's time to make a clean break and develop an expectancy of enough! In Matthew's Gospel, Jesus rebukes the scribes and the Pharisees as hypocrites because of their outward appearances of sanctity while harboring sinful desires within. Jesus said it was not sufficient to observe the letter of the law, but one must go deeply to the root and pull out from within "the desires of extortion and intemperance" which may lead to serious sin.

Avoiding sin is a good start. Actively changing the interior landscape of our thoughts and desires, moving away from anything in our being that takes us back to our past, is better protection from setbacks. Daily prayer, Scripture and devotions to Jesus, asking for grace and protection, complements the tool kit to speed us along on our journey to holiness.

Lord, I want to be a saint and witness for You in my lifetime. As You taught us to pray, we ask, "Lead us not into temptation, but deliver us from evil," so that one day we may share in Your glory in heaven.

Jesus, talk to me, talk to my spirit;
Jesus, speak to me, speak to my heart!

Using Our Talents for the Greater Glory of God

When I was a young teenager in the early 1960s the music of the Beatles hit the U.S. airwaves, and I was quickly mesmerized by their sound and their fame. For a long time I wanted to play in a band, or so I thought. While living away in a high school seminary, studying for the priesthood in Savannah in the mid to late 1960s, we formed garage bands and tried to grow our hair like the Beatles, which just wasn't going to be permitted with our seminary rector. Fortunately, the bands were acceptable, with names like "The Agents" and later "The

Common Cold," although we were designated to play mostly for the nursing home "circuit" in the Savannah area. I was a drummer, and we played and sang our music to our mostly elderly audience as if they were kids our age.

My desire to become a wanna-be rock star didn't sit well with my mother, who tried to discourage me, instead telling me to "seek first the kingdom of God"(see Matthew 6:33). I didn't understand then what one had to do with the other. Meanwhile, my musical "career" was soon over, the seminary closed in my junior year of high school, and my religious vocation remained in discernment until many years later when I pursued a Lay Carmelite vocation.

The news of Gregg Allman's death reminded me of my mother's concerns about rock and roll as a career. I really liked the Allman Brothers' band and their music. Yet the fate of the band members, including drummer Butch Trucks, who committed suicide, and now Gregg Allman, apparently dying from complications of liver disease, reminded me that not all is glamour in the music business. Gregg had been through five marriages and struggled with drug addictions. With so much fame and fortune, so many of the rock stars of my generation have relied on the world to provide what they needed, instead of making God their priority.

All this reminds me that talents are gifts from God, not for our own edification, but for use in service to God's kingdom. To understand the divine will and purpose for our lives and talents requires more than identifying as a Christian as if subscribing to a religion. To truly discern how we are to use God's gifts requires experiencing the love of Jesus on a personal level. When our faith and love begin to transform our minds, wills and hearts, causing us to set aside selfish desires and seeking instead to serve God, we become born again. The Holy Spirit provides the direction, the zeal and the determination to use our talents to serve others and perhaps help save a soul or two in the process.

With Pentecost Sunday a week from today, may we all be energized in our faith so we may spread the good news that forgiveness of our sins is now possible and life everlasting in heaven is within our grasp, due to the cross, death, and resurrection of Jesus.

They Will Know We Are Christians by Our Love

"By this all men will know that you are my disciples, if you love one another" (John 13:35).

"Love is patient, love is kind. It does not envy, it does not boast, it is not proud. It does not dishonor others, it is not self-seeking, it is not easily angered, it keeps no record of wrongs. Love does not delight in evil but rejoices with the truth. It always protects, always trusts, always hopes, always perseveres" (1 Corinthians 13:4-7).

Here are some commentary and insights around the inauguration speech. The new president spoke to what is wrong with America, calling out problems with crime, poverty, crumbling infrastructure, terrorism, which resonated with many Americans who supported Donald Trump. By dealing with America's brokenness via sheer grit, determination and patriotism, Trump promises a renewal of our country's greatness, and that's his good news.

The promise of renewed greatness fell flat with those who have opposed Trump and perhaps others who believe "Make America Great Again" may hark back to earlier times, with less focus on civil rights and more attention to the wealthy and affluent. Among these groups there is also fear of authoritarian rule which might trample over rights guaranteed by the Constitution.

When Jesus began His public ministry, His words caused quite a stir among the religious and public authorities of His time. His proclaiming that the last shall be first, and the first, last; that what comes out of a man's mouth is more important than what his mouth consumes; and that the Sabbath was made for man and not man for the Sabbath, evoked fear, anger and confusion. In response, the establishment went on the attack and was not satisfied until the Son of Man was crucified.

One of the more profound assertions coming from Jesus was His condensing of the commandments to two key requirements around our love of God with our whole heart, soul and mind and loving our neighbors as ourselves (Matthew

22:37-39). However people responded to Jesus, it was irrefutable that love was the driving force in the mission of Christ to give good news to all people that salvation was within reach, with peace and joy to follow.

Some wonder if love of country and all citizens is fueling the hard tone of the new president or are pride, pettiness and self-centeredness key drivers. Time will tell, and we all need to be prayerful in the meantime. We must be mindful that the new administration will be appointing Supreme Court justices, and the new president has gone on record as having a greater respect for life, particularly life that begins at conception. Despite concerns over ego and self-interests, we have a unique opportunity with the new president to solidify religious liberties, restore traditional family values and strengthen core values which made America great.

As the apostle Paul reminded us, in whatever we do we must have love and act in love, or our speech is reduced to so much rhetoric, the noise of a clanging cymbal. We will essentially fall flat in our efforts to win minds and hearts to embrace the love of Jesus, which makes all things possible (see 1 Corinthians 13:1-7).

Let us pray that President Trump will be prayerful and that love of God and love of neighbor will be a major influencer in the governing of our nation.

Bloom Where You Are Planted

A good corollary to last Sunday's "Being Present in the Moment" reflection is to manifest God's will in your life, in the majesty of the moment, "blooming where you are planted." The idea here is not to use catch phases or clichés to make a point. Instead the idea is to springboard from a world view of making the most of each day, with each encounter mostly for our own edification, to an awareness that God works in the now, blessing us and enabling us to accomplish great things for His kingdom.

God Is Present—Right Now: The power of the present was illuminated when Jesus was challenged by the Jews for asserting that father Abraham rejoiced in the coming of the Savior. Jesus responded to the Jews, who were incredulous that Jesus could have seen Abraham, by asserting His divinity, which transcends all time, saying, "Very truly I tell you"…"before Abraham was born, I am!" (see John 8:58). For me the "I am" speaks to the present, as God is with us in the here and now. The reality of an omnipresent God, engaged in every aspect of our lives, particularly the "right now," calls us to optimize each day.

Prepare for God's Blessings: I recall a famous Supreme Court justice speaking to the advice of his grandfather, who shared with him as a young man to "walk like you're going somewhere" even if you had no important destination. The lesson here is that we should live each day with a spring in our step, displaying a confidence that all is under control, even when doubts and uncertainty might be gnawing at our spirits. Our confidence should be grounded, not based on current circumstances that foretell a prosperous future, rather in spite of future uncertainties. Through our Christian faith we believe Jesus has our best interests at heart, which is enough to foretell that our trust in God and obedience to His commandments will ultimately provide for our needs, bringing peace and joy. Everything may not turn out to our liking, but we will be fine.

Bloom in Unlikely Places: Consider that the apostle Paul wrote one of his inspired letters that became part of sacred Scripture while in jail (see Philemon). Paul could have chosen to complain that prison conditions were just not conducive to good writing and shut down his work until circumstances improved. Instead, he bloomed where he was planted.

Get Started Now: We have opportunities *today* to give thanks to God for so many blessings, including the grace to do amazing things in our lives, while bringing the good news of salvation to our neighbors. Let's not find excuses, saying we will get started when completing school, after landing a better job, resolving family challenges or when slowing down or feeling better. While circumstances may not be the most conducive or opportunistic, go ahead and "bloom where you are planted" today, knowing God—"I am"—is with us right now, showering us with blessings and graces to help us face whatever challenges us, fulfilling God's will and purpose for our lives, with confidence and joy!

Acquiring More; Enjoying Less

> "Jesus answered (the rich young man), 'If you want to be perfect, go, sell your possessions and give to the poor, and you will have treasure in heaven. Then come, follow me.' When the young man heard this, he went away sad, because he had great wealth. Then Jesus said to his disciples, 'Truly I tell you, it is hard for someone who is rich to enter the kingdom of heaven. Again I tell you, it is easier for a camel to go through the eye of a needle than for someone who is rich to enter the kingdom of heaven'" (Matthew 19:21-23).

Last weekend, my wife Stephanie and I travelled to a car show in South Carolina. On a hot Saturday afternoon, we viewed all types of classic cars and particularly liked a 1955 Thunderbird on display. Having purchased a few vintage cars in the past, I began to ponder how I might invest some retirement savings to buy that orange 1968 Camaro that had a for-sale sign on the windshield. It wasn't long before I came to my senses, knowing the purchase might bring some momentary pleasure and also recalling how difficult it is to find a buyer when the allure of the classic car had passed. My bubble had burst, but it was okay.

Such is the story when we seek gratification in food, drink, clothing and other things we desire, enjoying the good feelings that follow and often wanting more and more. Having one classic car is terrific, so why not add a Model A Ford to the collection or consider building a garage to house several cars? And so it goes: We never seem to get enough of a good thing, as life can become an endless pursuit of pleasure and gratification.

Contrast the lust for stuff with the admonition of Jesus that "those of you who do not give up everything you have cannot be My disciples" (Luke 13:33). While it's great to have nice things, a cool car, nice home and maybe even a beach house, our treasure may in fact be placed in the things of this world and less in the kingdom of heaven. So it may be far better to learn to do with less, practicing self-denial and striving to be more content with what we have.

Donald Trump might take issue with the premise of having less in this world, and thereby gaining more in the next. My guess is that Trump, behind the extreme self-confidence and bluster, has reached his own level of diminishing returns with the wealth-happiness equation. Despite the daily media frenzy over the latest outrageous statement coming from Trump, I trust that at some level, the hand of God is present, providing inspiration and direction to the president and his leadership. At the same time, we must all pray that the power of Satan be kept at bay, to avoid irreparable harm to our nation from those who would do harm to our country for the sake of political expediency.

Instead of flexing our spending power to acquire more, let's exercise self-discipline. Allow the love of God and love of neighbor to have a greater influence in what we do, thereby finding God's will and purpose for our lives in service to others. As disciples of Jesus, we need very little material wealth along our journeys, instead trusting in divine providence to see that our needs and some wants are met (see Luke 9: 3). We may not stand as tall in the eyes of the world, but our reward in heaven will be greater.

> "St. Michael the Archangel, defend us in battle. Be our defense against the wickedness and snares of the devil. May God rebuke him, we humbly pray, and do thou, O Prince of the heavenly hosts, by the power of God, thrust into hell Satan and all the evil spirits, who prowl about the world seeking the ruin of souls. Amen" (Catholic prayer for protection from Satan).

Parable of the Talents—Discovering God's Purpose in Our Lives

> "For whoever has will be given more, and they will have abundance. Whoever does not have, even what they have will be taken from them" (Matthew 13:12).

God gives each of us talents, or special gifts, which are tied to His divine purpose for us. But it often takes some measure of courage and self-denial to unlock the full potential of His beneficence to be made manifest through us.

Having worked for many years in human resources in a hospital setting, I have had the opportunity to see first-hand the talents of nurses, therapists, cooks, housekeepers and others in various direct patient care and support roles. When conducting new employee orientation, one of the first things I do is emphasize the importance of work as more than a job, elevating what we do to a calling, a means of fulfilling our life's purpose in a special way. I always ask for personal stories from the newly minted employees, with several typically raising their hands, providing example after example of a calling to service. These stories sometimes come from a personal experience, such as agonizing when witnessing a loved one who suffered during an illness or being inspired by a family member who became a role model, choosing a life of service.

My purpose in asking new team members to share their inspiration for their occupational calling is certainly to recognize and celebrate their uniqueness in front of their peers. But it is also to inspire all who are present to unlock some passion, that untapped potential, which may require some emotional connection and stimulation to bring into full bloom. By acknowledging the uniqueness of every person, we help bring a measure of individual greatness into fruition.

When Jesus shared His parable about the master entrusting talents to his servants, of course this had a broader application, with talents encompassing all we are given, including our skills, our children or potential for children, our spouses, our wealth and so forth. Gifts are granted, not to be squandered for selfish purposes, but to manifest the goodness of God in service to our families, our neighbors and our communities.

For example, having a talent that produces wealth also provides an opportunity to help the poor. As a young married couple contemplates having children, being open to having a large family may require sacrifice to career pursuits and forsaking material possessions. The master who scolds the servant who buried his single talent illustrates the lost opportunity when we allow God's full potential for our lives, to lie dormant, underutilized or merely diverted for an easier, less challenging or more comfortable worldly existence.

Father, each of us has something special You have entrusted to us. Perhaps this blessing is to care for the less fortunate, to reveal some artistic ability or to display a knack for building things. Maybe our blessing is some affliction or difficulty, which we might overcome as an example to others. Today, may we discover the full potential of all You have bestowed on our lives, to use not so much for our own benefit but to support the work of Your kingdom, through Your Son, Jesus, we pray, amen.

Greatness Lies Within

At some level, we are all drawn to a deeper understanding of what God intended for our lives. What and whom we encounter invariably causes us to look for some connection to why we are in the world, believing that life must be more than a series of random interactions and events. To think otherwise tends to diminish the quality and meaningfulness of our existence and can cheapen whatever value we perceive flows from our words and actions.

Some will mentally construct a tapestry of accomplishments, believing success comes from their own intellect or brilliance. Others will recognize the folly of self-reliance, seeing the shortcomings which have followed, and instead consider that a higher power or authority must be in control, and perhaps a purpose and direction emanates from this source. As Christians, we should see only one source, the preeminence of Jesus Christ, who saved us from destruction due to our foibles, laying out a pathway to everlasting life and an inner peace in knowing salvation is possible.

For many Christians, keeping focused on the kingdom of God means being buffeted by Satan, who seems to grow more determined to thwart us, the closer we are to a credible and sustainable walk with Christ. This prince of doubt, this purveyor of self-reliance, promising us worldly fulfillment in the absence of God, will invariably leave us lacking, even despondent. We are taught in the New Testament that we have to put on the full armor of Christ's love and protection to minimize Satan's influence.

Amid our struggles in wanting to favor good over evil, we have to come to terms with our human frailties, accepting some degree of falling short of perfection, while keeping our eyes on the hereafter, knowing there may be some inconsistencies in our walk, even when death comes knocking. The idea of purgatory, where good intentions and reality intersect, where all is not lost, yet some purgation or cleansing is required before entering the kingdom, gives us hope that heaven is reachable and keeps despondency, due to our tendency to sinfulness, from taking hold.

Now we are ready to more fully realize God's purpose for our lives. Joy can replace despair, and, living more in the present, we can better see life unfolding before us, thereby allowing the presence of God's mercy and kindness to flow through our thoughts, words and actions. Thus, we are better prepared to see God in the smiles and struggles of our neighbor, encouraging all to see the good things and gifts uniquely manifesting in their lives through the love of God.

Our call to greatness in the eyes of God begins with a realization that brokenness is a human condition that can only be overcome with a total reliance on the love and healing grace and mercy of God. The Son of God, Christ Jesus, gave His life to free us from sin debt and enable sanctification and eternal life in heaven.

> "Then Jesus said to his disciples, 'Whoever wants to be my disciple must deny himself and take up his cross and follow me. For whoever wants to save his life will lose it, but whoever loses his life for me will find it'" (Matthew 16:24-25).

Contemporary Parenting and the Parable of the Prodigal Son

> "And the son said to him, 'Father, I have sinned against heaven and against you; I am no longer worthy to be called your son.' But the father said to his servants, 'Quick! Bring quickly the best robe, and put it on him; and put a ring on his finger and sandals on his feet. Bring the fattened calf and kill it. Let's have a feast and celebrate. For this my son of mine was dead, and is alive again; he was lost and is found.' So they began to celebrate." (see Luke 15:21-25).

I am afraid the well-intentioned father at the heart of the parable of the wayward son might not hold up well to the scrutiny of modern-day psychologists. In the parable the dad's unconditional love and really big welcome home for the son, who blew through his money and cavorted with unsavory people, would likely be viewed with suspicion. Yes, Dad might be seen as a naïve enabler of a manipulative son who takes advantage of his father's generosity, has his fill of food then is likely to be back on the road, even selling the ring Dad had put on his hand.

In fact, as a parent, I have heard it all, including it's all about boundaries and conditions when dealing with errant sons and daughters. After making a mess of things, if one of these adult kids comes knocking, saying "I'm sorry" (is probably out of money too), you're a "chump" of a parent if you respond positively, without requiring finding a job or working off a debt or something else, like attending Mass, as a condition of your mercy, and for opening your wallet again.

Please excuse the cynicism. In practice, it has always been difficult for me to hold fast to conditions. That's because my love for family is indeed unconditional and doesn't always hold up well to preconditioned hard and fast rules.

So the parable of the prodigal son is not so much a lesson in contemporary parenting but serves as a reminder that the boundless love and mercy of our heavenly Father transcends boundaries and conditions. God the Father gave us His only Son to atone for our sins, and He forgives and forgets unceasingly, despite our propensity to mess up again and again.

Now if we turn our backs on God and stubbornly stick to our wayward behaviors, God will allow us to remain in rebellion. After all, the father of the prodigal didn't go looking for the son. When the son was ready to amend his ways, he returned to a loving father, just as our heavenly Father will lovingly accept us back, over and over, when we turn to Him.

This is about the hope of salvation, which we all desperately need. Like my Father in heaven, who can't not love me, I can't not love my children and grandchildren. This is where good parenting intersects with the wisdom of the parable of the prodigal son.

> "I will give you a new heart and put a new spirit in you; I will remove from you your heart of stone and give you a heart of flesh" (Ezekiel 36:26).

Living Out Our Christian Witness

> "And whoever does not carry their cross and follow me cannot be my disciple...In the same way, those of you who do not give up everything you have cannot be my disciple" (Luke 14:27, 33).

> "All these things I have kept", the young man said. "What do I still lack?" Jesus answered, "If you want to be perfect, go, sell your possessions and give to the poor, and you will have treasure in heaven. Then, come, follow me." When the young man heard this, he went away sad, because he had great wealth" (Matthew 19:20-22).

With shoppers out in force hunting Black Friday sales, which had been moved back to the evening of Thanksgiving, the Christmas shopping season is in full swing. Looking for the best deal on a 50" HDTV or grabbing some other electronic device before the supply is exhausted, it's easy to get swept away with the excitement and anticipation of gift-giving and spirited family gatherings.

Against this festive backdrop we have daily reports and images on cable news of ongoing demonstrations over the tragic shooting death of a Black teen in Ferguson, Missouri, with many believing justice was not done in the recent grand jury decision. Frustrations in this community swirl around the reality of high unemployment, particularly among minority youth, with hopelessness taking root as confidence in a prosperous future seems beyond reach for so many. To make matters worse, sinister influences and forces of evil are capitalizing on the unrest, adding violence and destruction to the mix, making it even more challenging for reasonable people to come together to find common ground in addressing legitimate concerns.

In the comfort of our relative prosperity we can sit back and make judgments about bad choices, broken families and the influences of the culture glamorizing drugs and violence. At our holiday gatherings we might opine that what's needed is zero tolerance for the criminal element and a stronger police presence and then proceed to make value judgments about the demonstrators and their life circumstances.

We should first reflect on our Christian witness, knowing Jesus would have been at home in Ferguson, ministering to those who just can't get beyond what happened this past week, giving hope that all things can be made new again through the cleansing power and love of God. Jesus would preach love, redemption, lifting up those who are marginalized and leaving the righteous so He can pursue the lost sheep to save their souls.

Jesus made it clear what is necessary to be His disciple. His admonition to give up everything we have lays down fairly strong requirements for true discipleship. For many believers, this may be the dividing point that separates Christians who give of themselves only when convenient and others who are willing to put all on the line, including their lives, careers and all they possess for Jesus.

Renouncing all we have means not allowing anything to separate us from the love of Christ. Anything that preoccupies our lives, including money, possessions, careers, egos, feelings of superiority and unhealthy relationships, is suspect. Those things that distract us from our capacity to seek first the kingdom of God and all His righteousness likely should be minimized or renounced completely.

Applying the test to our own lives, if we find ourselves more self-dependent, more taken by the allure of what we possess and value in this world, rather than by our pursuit of what pleases God, then I would recommend going deeper into prayer and self-denial and quieting down our lives. Go a day or two without television, music and social media, allowing your spirit to calm down some. Try being completely still and enable the Holy Spirit to dwell within your mind and heart. Empty yourself of any pretense of importance, acknowledging we are nothing without the infinite love of Jesus. In this stillness perhaps God's unique plan for your life in helping bring the good news of salvation, peace and joy to the world can be revealed. As your heart draws even closer to the love of Jesus, a calm and peace may begin to reside in your spirit. Thus, in a more profound way, Christ lives in you.

> "I came that they might have life and have it
> more abundantly" (John 10:10). (NKJV)

Back to the turmoil in Ferguson: Rather than pointing a finger in judgment, perhaps we should be more in prayer, asking God to bring healing to these communities, including our own, and to our nation. Consider how you and I would fare, with our past misjudgments and moral failings exposed, if today we were held to account before our Creator. When it comes to gaining life everlasting, the truth is that we all fall short but for the undeserved grace flowing from the shed blood of Jesus at Calvary and made complete by His resurrection.

Being more Christ-like may mean becoming advocates for social justice, promoting economic opportunities in our communities for the disadvantaged, stressing education and supporting intact families. Christian churches should be at the forefront in driving these changes.

Following the example of Jesus, we must lead with love, stressing the sanctity of life from conception, encouraging families with both mother and father present and promoting marriage as the sacred bond between a man and a woman. While the vocal disciples of secular culture may scoff at us as being out of touch or irrelevant, we must stand firm, asking God for strength and perseverance to follow His commandments and bring souls to His kingdom.

Father, grant me the grace and courage to go deeper into my relationship with You, finding greater intimacy with Jesus and growing a greater sense of confidence in my daily walk. I want to serve You and manifest Your goodness and healing love in my words and actions. Through the prayerful intercession of your Son, Jesus, grant me protection from the evil one so I might move even quickly to the higher purpose You have called me to, in order to help save souls for Your kingdom.

Come, Holy Spirit, talk to me, talk to my spirit,
Come, Holy Spirit, speak to me, speak to my heart!

In Our Imperfections, God's Power Finds Perfection

"But He said to me, "My grace is sufficient for you, for my power is made perfect in weakness." Therefore I will boast all the more gladly about my weaknesses, so that Christ's power may rest on me . That is why, for Christ's sake, I delight in weaknesses, in insults, in hardships, in persecutions, in difficulties. For when I am weak, then I am strong" (2 Corinthians 12:9-10).

The apostle Paul wrote so eloquently of the struggles we as Christians face each day, in fending off temptations, rebuking Satan and striving to live good and holy lives. Paul keenly understood this, writing in 2 Corinthians about his own spiritual growth. He cautioned about becoming too elated in heavenly revelations and visions and that God gave him "a thorn in the flesh," an "angel of Satan," to torment him as a reminder of his own human frailty and his absolute dependence on the love of Jesus to sustain him. In response to Paul's plea to remove his thorn, whether that be some human weakness, unrelenting temptation or tendency to sinfulness, God responded that His "grace is sufficient" to overcome what can be an unrelenting pull toward despair and rebellion.

Instead of throwing up his hands in frustration, Paul, being filled with the Holy Spirit, understood the divine connection, exclaiming that the power of Christ is made perfect in his weaknesses. In simple terms, Jesus gives hope to all of us by helping us overcome our tendency to anger, for example, or warming our hearts to show care and concern to neighbors who might have offended us in some way. Through His infinite love Jesus extends grace to us each day, enabling us to manifest His goodness, despite our sinful nature, for the salvation of souls, starting with our own.

It should give us some consolation that the Bible has ample examples of God's lifting up some pretty wretched and broken people to do the most amazing work for His kingdom. Remember that the apostle Paul was in the business of killing Christians, until Jesus entered his life in a most dramatic way, striking him to the ground, helping transform his heart to serve and not persecute Christians.

The whole band of the original twelve apostles, hand-picked by Jesus, had lots of issues, including in their group a former tax collector and a traitor who would self-select out. Of course, their leader was a headstrong, excitable character named Peter, who ran for cover when Jesus faced crucifixion and denied knowing Him three times. Prone to preoccupations like arguing who was the greatest among their lot, the apostles were chosen by Jesus to take His message of love and salvation to all nations. Whatever personal baggage and hang-ups they possessed, once Pentecost brought the fire of the Holy Spirit upon their minds and hearts, they became hardcore in their zeal, love and determination to preach Christ crucified and risen from the dead to all who would listen.

> "But God chose the foolish things of this world to shame the wise, and God chose the weak things of the world to shame the strong" (1 Corinthians 1:27).

Knowing the apostles overcame their depravity through the grace of God to do amazing work and endure persecutions in order to advance the church of Jesus Christ, this is a message of hope to all struggling Christians. In our own spiritual journeys we must come to terms with our sinful tendencies, asking for God's forgiveness and amending our lives, realizing we never completely shed our inclinations to rebel against God. That spiritual "pebble in our shoe" should keep us humble, reminding us of our complete dependence on the love of Jesus and helping us keep our gaze on Him each day.

Father, thank You for Your many blessings, particularly my own imperfections, knowing Your will and purpose for my life are made manifest through my talents and even my shortcomings. Help me to come to terms with my weaknesses, particularly those unrelenting thorns in the flesh. I pray for grace not to be overcome by evil. I also realize my insufficiencies are a blessing as I am desperately in need of Your love to bolster me against my depravity, enabling me to do great things for Your kingdom.

> Jesus, talk to me, talk to my spirit,
> Jesus, speak to me, speak to my heart!

Finding Reconciliation with a Suffering Christ

> "Finally, be strong in the Lord and in his mighty power. "Put on the full armor of God, so that you can take your stand against the devil's schemes. For our struggle is not against flesh and blood, but against the rulers, against the authorities, against the powers of this dark world and against the spiritual forces of evil in the heavenly realms" (Ephesians 6: 10-12)

Last week I stood in line for around twenty minutes at a penance service at the Cathedral of Christ the King in Atlanta. I was impressed with the long lines as I waited for my turn to make my confession. It just makes sense to get my spiritual house in order, particularly during Holy Week, to unload any baggage due to my own spiritual lapses, allowing me to draw closer to the crucified and risen Christ.

My peculiar sensibilities lead me to a conclusion that God's mission and purpose for my life cannot be perfected until I come to terms with any barriers, which means anything that gets in the way of my becoming a suitable vessel, a credible instrumentality for the work of our Lord. I don't consider this vanity, but more about integrity, knowing I can't have one foot in a life of disordered affections, including unhealthy attachments to people and possessions, or lust, pride or self-sufficiency, and the other foot in the spiritual realm, pursuing God's will. It's sort of like the new wine leaking out of, and not compatible with, old wineskins, as Jesus spoke about in one of His parables. If having integrity in seeking to do God's will is the new wine but kept in the old wineskins of unresolved sinfulness, the two will be incompatible, and integrity will soon leach away and be lost.

Humility informs me, and my past history reminds me that spiritual integrity is not easily acquired or maintained but for an outpouring of grace from God. I believe Satan relishes the thought of tripping up a believer who is actually making a little headway as a committed Christian. Yes, the tests and trials will come. And only when we yield to God, saying, "I just can't do this—I give it all to You, Lord," can we begin to resist the undertow of our natural tendencies toward the bad stuff of life. As a Catholic, I know the Sacrament of Reconciliation unlocks God's mercy and forgiveness, unburdening me of the weight of my sins, again and again. Regularly partaking of the Sacrament of the Holy Eucharist, receiving the real presence, the body, blood, soul and divinity of Christ, provides me spiritual sustenance to help keep me strong, enabling me to put on the full armor of God's protection.

If this sounds like the spiritual warfare you've heard about, you're right on target. Beyond battling our own demons, we also are confronted with the culture of death. We are being pressured more and more to compromise our beliefs, to acknowledge that life in the womb, when unwanted, can be snuffed out and life outside the womb, if feeble or lacking due to pain or deformity, might be ended for the common good. In the name of tolerance and protecting civil rights, we are being intimidated to accept a redefinition of marriage, lest we be called bigots. Yes, the storm clouds are forming where our faith, our spiritual integrity, may be sorely tested.

The message of Holy Week is that Jesus conquered death due to sin through His suffering and death at Calvary and then His resurrection, in body and spirit, which we celebrate on Easter Sunday. Jesus opened the door to eternal life, providing us a means to becoming reconciled with Him and the grace to defeat the flesh and to stand tall against Satan and the principalities and powers, knowing we can therefore claim victory in heaven!

The Pursuit of Happiness—How Do We Get There?

It's interesting to ponder those aspects of our lives we consider as indispensable to our happiness. What comes to mind is our family, faith, necessities of daily living and a few material things we desire and enjoy.

This sounds about right, until you get down the path of a closer walk with Christ. Following the disciplines of daily prayer and devotions and becoming increasingly aware of God's presence in our lives, a transformation can occur. Needs and wants may become less the object of our lives; instead we enjoy the fruits that flow from a life of pursuing God's will. We begin to sense our true poverty but for God's grace, forgiveness and redemption.

Happiness, derived from a closer walk with Christ, can bring about a peace and calm, knowing God's love and grace are more than enough. Having this, we need nothing else!

We can better understand the admonition of Jesus that we must renounce all we have in order to be His disciples. It's not that we must literally sell everything we own and become paupers for Jesus. Instead, when seeking first the kingdom of God and all His righteousness, all else is added, tending to our needs and even some wants.

With a sharper focus on God in our daily lives, worldly pursuits become less alluring. When freed from the unrelenting pursuit of things, our spirits are calmed, allowing pure happiness to flow through us.

Father, may my happiness be derived from being faithful to Your will and purpose for me and less dependent upon accumulating things, achieving success and gaining worldly affirmation and approval. Remind me of Mother Teresa's inspired message that I am here, not to be successful, but to be faithful. Your love and grace are more than sufficient!

Jesus, talk to me, talk to my spirit;
Jesus, speak to me, speak to my heart.

Personal Success or Struggle, Without Love, Gains Nothing

"If I speak in the tongues of men and angels, but do not have love, I am only a resounding gong or a clanging cymbal. And if I have the gift of prophecy and can fathom all mysteries and all knowledge, and I have a faith that can move mountains, but do not have love, I am nothing. If I give all I possess to the poor and give over my body to hardship that I may boast, but do not have love, I gain nothing"

"Love is patient, love is kind. It does not envy, it does not boast, it is not proud. It does not dishonor others, it is not self-seeking, it is not easily angered, and it keeps no record of wrongs. Love does not delight in evil but rejoices with the truth. It always protects, always trusts, always hopes, and always perseveres" (1 Corinthians 13: 1-7).

Jesus loved us so much, and unconditionally, that He gave His precious life for us on the cross.

He wants us to love Him, to save our souls, but doesn't demand it. He doesn't require our love for Him as a response to His personal sacrifice on the cross. Jesus invites us to a simpler, more fulfilling life, by loving God and our neighbor and seeking first His kingdom in all we do. Our Christian faith informs us that love of God and neighbor is indispensable to achieve salvation.

Unconditional love requires giving something of value to another person, who could be someone we care about or even a complete stranger, without any expectation of receiving any favor or love in return. This tends to be easier for parents to their children because of a parent's deep and natural bond for a son or daughter. Often times, giving love to another may be more difficult, particularly for a person we don't care for or who doesn't care for us. Jesus tells us we must love our neighbors as ourselves, without any condition or requirement of being worthy of love.

The intentional action to serve God's kingdom through works of kindness and compassion is complete in the eyes of God, irrespective of the impact made or appreciation shown by the recipient. In other words, our concern should be to lift up our neighbor, showing love and mercy, leaving the saving of souls to God.

When Paul preaches love as a test of true commitment to Jesus, he takes the challenge of unconditional love to another level. In life, we can accomplish great things and suffer many indignities, which may be noteworthy, yet fall short in the eyes of God if we do not have love for one another. Works without love are diminished. Think of the following life experiences and consider how these would be lacking but for love and selflessness:

*We give to the poor, making a personal sacrifice, and do it anonymously.

*We might suffer from illness or ridicule yet remain positive, giving encouragement to another who may be downtrodden.

*We might achieve acclaim in our work yet remain humble and sign up to provide career counseling and coaching to those who have lost their jobs.

*We may be blessed with a beautiful family and successful children and decide to adopt a special needs child.

*We might acquire material wealth; yet as Christians we become dispossessed of the hold riches may have on our lives, yearning to desire nothing but to serve God's kingdom, putting all we have at His disposal.

If we're prone to telling others about our good fortune or disappointments, only to brag or to proclaim our "victim-ness" about what life has brought us, that is not love. Achieving much, yet turning our backs on a brother or sister in need, is not love. When God has given us much, and we ridicule others who may appear to have received less, our lack of compassion greatly diminishes the value of God's gifts.

Love means giving all the credit to Jesus, understanding that even suffering may be permitted for the salvation of our souls. In all things, positive or negative, we cannot allow our life experience to blunt the care and concern we are expected to have for our neighbor. By focusing on love of God and love for one another, we can help all aspire to receive the same joy and peace we endeavor to achieve through our closer walk with Jesus.

Father, today, please make me aware of opportunities to serve my neighbor. Thank You for the many blessings You have bestowed on me. Whether I am joyful or sorrowful, empower me to perform works of mercy and kindness with a cheerful spirit and without any expectations. May I use Your gifts for the benefit of those You place in my path. Because I love You, I do all for You, giving You all the glory and praise, through the name of Your Son, Jesus, I pray, amen!

Choosing between Light and Darkness

"If we claim to have fellowship with Him and yet walk in the darkness, we lie and do not live out the truth. But if we walk in the light, as He is in the light, we have fellowship with one another, and the blood of Jesus, His Son, purifies us from all sin" (1 John 1:6-7).

"So you also must be ready, because the Son of Man will come at an hour when you do not expect Him" (Matthew 24:44).

Living a good and holy life requires constant vigilance as you're never out of the fight against the influence of powers and principalities. I was reminded of that yesterday by a nice man who works in the service department at a local car dealership where I get my oil changed. As we were taking about our faith, he told me that the evil one, Satan, "has to eat too" and is always on duty looking to derail a well-meaning Christian.

In achieving some measure of sustainability in our walk with Christ, we must decide daily to choose to follow the light and not the darkness. We are fooling ourselves if our commitment is inconsistent or even half-hearted. Carrying around unconfessed serious sin is problematic, maybe because we haven't decided to turn completely away from darkness, but we're thinking about it. Our lukewarm approach to achieving holiness may leave us lacking should we be called to account today in eternity.

Maybe we have allowed our lives to become too cluttered with our worldly cares, possessions and concerns. Does Christ live within us, or have we subconsciously pushed Christ over to the side, as we go about our days visibly carrying our worries and anxieties on our shoulders and finding solace in telling our friends and family about our burdens. Is there a good measure of joy in our lives, or do we spend more time lamenting over our losses and what could have been? Are we present in the moment, being thankful for our many blessings, or are we preoccupied with yesterday's disappointments and tomorrow's worries?

Trust, Obey, Listen and Rejoice—Today!

Today is a good day to renew our complete and unequivocal **trust** in God's love and mercy while placing an eviction notice on anything that seems to separate us from Christ. Today let's resolve to confess our sins, this time with a firm purpose of amendment, to **obey** God and follow His commandments.

Today let's stop talking so much and begin turning off our devices and finding quiet time and **listen**, so God may speak to our hearts and minds about His will, purpose and direction for us. As we empty ourselves of self-centeredness and preoccupations, taming our rebellious nature and ridding ourselves of any pretense of self-sufficiency, perhaps then we can **rejoice** and begin to experience a bit more joy, knowing our salvation in Christ Jesus is secure.

Parable of the Workers Sent to the Vineyard—A Lesson in Social Injustice or Something More?

> "The workers who were hired about five in the afternoon came, and each received a denarius. So, when those came who were hired first, they expected to receive more. But each one of them also received a denarius. When they received it, they began to grumble against the landowner. 'These who were hired last only worked one hour,' they said, 'and you have made them equal to us who have borne the burden of the work and the heat of the day'" (Matthew 20:9-12).

In 2018 a landowner who gives as much to the laborers coming late in the workday as those coming at the start of the day might face a legal challenge. Drawing from my human resources experience, I'd think someone needed to counsel the owner of the vineyard as to potential equal employment opportunity claims that might arise from his arbitrary pay practices.

Maybe Jesus had other ideas, having nothing to do with fairness nor espousing the unbridled right of a landowner to pay laborers in an unequal fashion. Perhaps the lesson here had more to do with the mercy of God.

When Jesus spent time with tax collectors, known sinners and others of ill repute, I expect a few of those watching, living righteous lives, wondered why they were not included.

Remember the brother of the prodigal son, so painfully dismayed that his father had made such a fuss over his crazy, misguided brother while doing little, it appeared, to celebrate his faithfulness and dependability.

> "'My son,' the father said, 'you are always with me, and everything I have is yours. But we had to celebrate and be glad, because this brother of yours was dead and is alive again; he was lost and is found'" (Luke 15:31-32).

> "I tell you that in the same way (compared to finding one lost sheep) there will be more rejoicing in heaven over one sinner who repents than over ninety-nine persons who do not." (Luke 15:7).

Going back to the issue of fairness, flowing from the parable of the laborers in the vineyard, we are reminded that Jesus did not take the form of a man to come to save the righteous, but to convert sinners, as potential lost souls. The business of salvation doesn't square with our contemporary notions of fairness and equality. A conversion of heart, confession of sin and securing eternal life may occur in a person who comes late to God's vineyard. The mercy of God allows the latecomer to receive salvation and experience eternal joy in the same measure, or perhaps more, than the steady, faithful servant of God who doesn't stray from living a good and holy life.

Because of this reality we should rejoice as the love of God sustains us when we follow His will. More important, this same love and mercy saves us from ourselves when we are rebellious in sin, knowing Jesus has always had an affinity for restoring the lost and broken. For this, we are even more hopeful that salvation is possible for all who sooner or later profess and live the cross and resurrection of Jesus.

Father, because You loved us You sent Your Son to dwell among us, to experience human joy and pain, and to give His life at Calvary and rise from the dead. All of this was done to save us from eternal damnation and make salvation and life eternal in heaven a reality. As we get up each day and take up our own crosses, may we see each encounter with our neighbor as an opportunity to extend the love of Christ and maybe help save one soul.

When I experience wretchedness in others, may I not feel any pride in my own righteousness, knowing it is only by the grace of God that I am spared the wrath of my own sinful tendencies. May I too rejoice when a life is transformed for Christ. Amen!

Making the Business Case for Living a Good and Holy Life as a Christian

> "God does not require that we be successful,
> only that we be faithful." —Mother Teresa

I recently watched an interview on YouTube involving business leaders and the founder of Tesla and SpaceX, Elon Musk. A famous billionaire, Musk, who is also considered by many to be like the Thomas Edison of our time, was asked about technology and the future. He foresees deep space travel and even colonization on far away planets.

When asked about life itself and what deeper meaning was possible in the future, Musk stuck to his focus on technology, artificial intelligence and man's untapped potential. There was no mention of God, man's limitations or the importance of one's soul in preparing for the future. The business case around realizing the full potential of technology and optimization of human potential did not include calling out our potential as spiritual beings, following God's will, where all things are possible.

Now I am not judging Elon Musk, and I may have missed in his remarks a reference to the power and majesty of God as an important influence. As I have googled Elon Musk I've found references to the incompatibility of religion with science as essentially governing what is possible and perhaps more measurable, in all things related to human potential. In this context spirituality is considered as too wrapped up in feelings, with possibilities considered as too speculative or unprovable and which otherwise often defy anything science can explain.

I disagree. After observing human behavior during my years as a human resources professional, I realized people need to be freed from their own inadequacies. I have seen people frustrated from their relentless pursuit of happiness on their own terms, looking to science, technology and human intellect to draw out and make all things possible. I believe all people possess a deep-down hankering for sustainable happiness in this life, a reason for being, a connection to something bigger than the limitations of their own sensibilities and skills. In this calculus, science and technology, driving human potential, come up short.

As true believers of Jesus Christ, we have found answers in the shed blood of our Savior, who answered questions about human potential and laid down a pathway to finding God's plan and our potential for our lives. Accepting the premise that we were all born needing salvation because of the sin of Adam, that our possibilities connect to a divine will, purpose and direction for our lives, we therefore look to Jesus as a means of rising above earthly and metaphysical limitations. The cross and resurrection redeemed us from damnation due to our tendencies toward sin and self-destruction and have made possible unimaginable possibilities. "I can do all things through him who gives me strength " (Philippians 4:13).

With love of God and neighbor as our guiding principle and practicing humility in knowing that but for Jesus we have no hope for everlasting life and would despair, we proceed with greater confidence. Putting the love of God as the true guide in our daily living, we look to serve our brothers and sisters in sharing the good news of salvation. Seeking first God's kingdom tends to simplify things, and being faithful to His commandments opens the door to more wholesome relationships and a simpler life, unencumbered with a mindless, relentless pursuit of things and good feelings, which often have no end other than endless attempts at self-gratification and happiness.

Making all we do subservient to the will of the Father and thus giving up control of our finances, our careers and our possibilities, the love of our Savior who will bolster us is more than sufficient. In return, we will live healthier and happier, a good business case, if you will, for living a good and holy life in Christ Jesus.

Father, we thank You for loving us so much that You sent Your only Son so we may truly have life, and life more abundant and full! We have the hope of salvation, and we must take this message to a world caught up in self-sufficiency and believing all things are possible through science, technology and human intelligence. It's not what we achieve, but it's about being faithful to God's will and purpose in which we find sustainable peace and joy. Send Your Holy Spirit to bolster us against the evil one and give us fortitude to take this good news of salvation to all people. Through the name of Jesus, we pray, amen.

What's It Going to Be: Sinner or Saint?

> "I know your deeds, that you are neither cold nor hot. I wish you were either one or the other! So, because you are lukewarm—neither hot nor cold—I am about to spit you out of my mouth" (Revelation 3:15-16).

"No one can serve two masters. Either you will hate the one and love the other, or you will be devoted to the one and despise the other." (Matthew 6:24).

When we make it a point to pray daily, attend church and serve our neighbor, no doubt we are reflecting our faith in God and living as Jesus taught us. We're on our way to salvation, right? Then what about those remaining things in our lives that may be incongruent to our pathway to heaven? Should we speak uncharitably about our neighbor, allow our thoughts to wander where they should not or not speak up when we see injustice? Are we bothered afterward that our thoughts or actions are out of step with our Christian walk? Are we often confessing acts of incongruence, asking for God's forgiveness and striving to amend our lives? If not, then maybe our aspirations of salvation are delusional.

Inevitably, a higher level of spiritual integrity will force us to close the gaps between a life of virtue and a more lukewarm existence, where we have one foot in the kingdom and the other in the junk of the world. The world and the kingdom of God just don't mix well as our life on earth is transitory, and sustainable happiness in this life is inevitably blunted, unless our primary focus is seeking God's kingdom, picking up our crosses daily and obeying His commandments.

Jesus had no use for "lukewarm" believers, those who pretended to serve the world and serve God. We too must realize that tepid Christians are set up for failure, understanding that the evil one, Satan, will more likely win out unless a Christian has both feet firmly planted in God's will and purpose.

Chapter 3

LISTEN

The "Big Bang" of Pentecost Sunday

"When the day of Pentecost came, they were all together in one place. Suddenly a sound like the blowing of a violent wind came from heaven and filled the whole house where they were sitting. They saw what seemed to be tongues of fire that separated and came to rest on each of them. All of them were filled with the Holy Spirit and began to speak in other tongues as the Spirit enabled them" (Acts 2:1-4).

"Anything worth doing is worth overdoing. Moderation is for cowards" (from the movie *Lone Survivor*).

The motion picture *Lone Survivor* tells the story of four Navy Seals who were on a special ops mission and became entrapped in the mountains of Afghanistan. Way outnumbered, the Seals had to bravely fight the encircling Taliban forces, using all of their survival skills against overwhelming odds in order to break free. Their all-in approach, anticipating extreme hardship and extraordinary effort beyond moderation, and not afraid to die, reminds me of the apostles of Pentecost. They were empowered through the Holy Spirit to take the good news message of Jesus Christ to all nations, despite having limited resources and facing certain opposition and persecution.

The gifts of Pentecost unlocked the passion, courage and sheer determination of a budding community of believers to do extraordinary things for God's kingdom. As the Holy Spirit descended upon the apostles, the result was like a "Big Bang," enabling in a massive way the spreading of the message of Christ as Savior of the world.

Imagine the apostles before Pentecost, gathered in the Upper Room, still somewhat bewildered over the events at Calvary, perhaps fearing persecution as followers of Christ and awaiting the Holy Spirit as Jesus had promised. On the day of Pentecost the Holy Spirit descended upon them, and amazing things began to happen. Beginning with Acts 4:2, the apostles Peter and John, being "unschooled and ordinary men," showed great courage in proclaiming the resurrection of Jesus in plain view of the elders and teachers of the Jewish law, inspiring about five thousand men to become believers.

In Acts 5, Peter, through the sheer power of the Holy Spirit, inspired people to bring their sick into the street and place them on beds and mats so Peter's shadow might fall on some as he passed them.

When the apostles were jailed by the Sadducees (see Acts 5:17-20), God's "special ops" team of angels released them under the noses of the guards and with the jail door remaining locked. Showing no moderation in his passion for Christ, Peter and his team were back on the streets, teaching the masses while standing in the temple courts. Then they were brought before the Sanhedrin for disobeying orders that they should not teach in the name of Jesus. The apostles were flogged, again ordered not to preach Jesus. The apostles ignored these warnings too, going from house to house, fearlessly proclaiming Jesus was the Messiah.

In Acts 12:3-23, King Herod jailed Peter for his ministry. Despite being bound with chains and asleep between two soldiers with sentries posted, Peter was nudged by an "angel of the Lord" to wake up and put on his cloak. He then walked out of the prison, right past the guards and through the iron gate leading into the city, which opened "by itself" for Peter. When Herod got word of the escape he ordered the guards to be executed. Soon afterward in an assembly, Herod refused to give praise to God, and the angel of the Lord struck him, causing Herod to be eaten by worms. Meanwhile, the preaching and healing ministry of the apostles continued in full force.

The legacy of the apostles is heavy with courage and fearlessness, instructing us to speak the truth, totally dependent on the Holy Spirit for inspiration, strength and perseverance in taking the salvation message to all people. Today more than ever we need the same relentlessness among Christians in standing up for truth, defending life and being uncompromising about the sanctity of marriage between one man and one woman. Like the apostles, we will be ridiculed and maybe face persecution although the Holy Spirit will bolster and sustain us for the journey.

Father, on this day of Pentecost, we ask that You send Your Holy Spirit to renew the hearts of Christians everywhere and strengthen their resolve as soldiers for Christ. The culture is in dire need of conversion as our level of determination and sole dependence on God is also in need of renewal. Give us courage and fearlessness so, like the apostles, we can speak openly about our faith, call out evil and proclaim Jesus as our only hope of salvation.

We adore You, O Christ, and we praise You, because by Your holy cross, death, and resurrection, and bolstered by the Holy Spirit, You have redeemed the world!

Is My Prayer Life Good Enough?

> "You, Lord, are forgiving and good, abounding in love to all who call to you. Hear my prayer, Lord; listen to my cry for mercy. When I am in distress, I call to you, because you answer me" (Psalm 86:5-7).

"Rejoice always, pray continually, give thanks in
all circumstances; for this is God's will for you in
Christ Jesus" (1 Thessalonians 5:16-18).

If prayer is indispensable to knowing God's plan for us for obtaining life everlasting, how then should a Christian seek a more effective prayer life? Should we pray more frequently, more fervently, more reverently? In our performance improvement culture, our spiritual lives are also subject to scrutiny, the same as our diet and exercise regimen. Perhaps a more structured and disciplined approach to our spiritual strengthening will net us a closer walk with Jesus, right?

In fact, prayer is a uniquely personal matter, as is our overall relationship with Jesus. Connecting prayer to eternity, the only measurement or metric that matters is the likelihood of spending eternity with Jesus, which is, of course, hard to know but for seeking God's kingdom first and all His righteousness. While no one has the perfect measuring stick, here are some thoughts on tuning up our prayers, in hopes of drawing closer to Christ.

Prayer can be spontaneous, a daily regimen, by rote or repetition. Prayer can be an expression of fear that bad things will happen but for the intercession of a merciful God. Prayer can be a way of expressing gratitude for many blessings we have received, including trials and hardships. Prayer can be a petition for protection, a favorable outcome or intercession, benefiting our family or our neighbor.

There is one more type of prayer I want to share with you. It's a variation of "prayer unceasing," as referenced in 1 Thessalonians, where your words and actions become an expression of love and communication with God. You're in a constant mindfulness of God's presence, in a quiet dialogue of sorts seeking guidance and direction to show you the way, to provide you with wisdom and strength, becoming a matter of almost routine consciousness. The dialogue can take on a partnership where you are always aware of God's presence, direction and blessings which you strive to apply each day. With thankfulness you anticipate the day's joys and sufferings and stand ready to receive revelations as God is with you and supporting you every step of the way.

Each day might begin with a simple prayer: "Lord, do with me as You will." Like the apostle Paul, perhaps one day we too can say, "I have been crucified with Christ and I no longer live, but Christ lives in me " (Galatians 2:20).

A Daily Spiritual Tune-Up

> "Do not be anxious about anything, but in every situation, by prayer and petition, with thanksgiving, present your requests to God. And the peace of God, which transcends all understanding, will guard your hearts and your minds in Christ Jesus. Finally, brothers and sisters, whatever is true, whatever is noble, whatever

is right, whatever is pure, whatever is admirable—if anything is excellent or praiseworthy—
think about such things" (Philippians 4:6-8).

"Then Jesus told His disciples, 'Whoever wants to
be my disciple must deny themselves and take
up their cross and follow me'"(Matthew 16:24).

Pursuing a closer walk with Jesus requires daily maintenance and vigilance. It seems that Satan works extra hard to trip up the committed believer who is striving each day to live a good and holy life. A struggle can ensue in which worldly cares and concerns can cause us to worry, and we forget Paul's instruction that we not "be anxious about anything," instead presenting our "requests to God."

Bombarded by images from our mass media, fueling a lust for possessions, prestige and all types of gratification, we can begin to believe all we need is within our grasp if we just work hard and make lots of money. After all, it's the American way, right? Unfortunately, and all too often, allowing our "wanting more" to dominate our lives can leave us lacking, irritable, more vulnerable to sin and hardly joyful.

To help keep us less self-centered and more focused on doing God's will, I would suggest making a routine of the following daily practices, which might be helpful:

1. Start each day with prayer, Scripture and meditation.

2. Examine our consciences, confess our sins and ask for forgiveness.

3. Seek God's direction, saying, "Lord, do with me as You will."

4. Practice being quiet, with less music, television or internet.

5. Practice self-denial, learning to live with less, instead giving more to help others.

6. Be less critical or judgmental. Bite our tongues, knowing we all fall short in the eyes of God.

7. Smile more, encourage more, even when we lack support and encouragement.

8. Seek opportunities to extend kindness and generosity to others.

9. Spend Sundays worshipping God and being with family and friends.

10. Remember that we are nothing and have nothing, except for the infinite love, mercy and promise of everlasting life through the suffering, death and resurrection of Christ.

Father, it's clear I can't do this spiritual journey without lots of help. Thank You for sending Your Son, Jesus, to save us from certain disaster by His supreme act of love, giving His life so we might gain everlasting life. I ask that You send Your Holy Spirit to bolster me, to guide me, to lift me when I'm down, so I can be better prepared to know and do Your will and thereby find an abundance of lasting peace and joy, amen.

You Can't Blend Your New Life with Old Habits

I read in Matthew's Gospel where Jesus teaches His apostles about the folly of pouring new wine into old wineskins or patching old ripped cloth with a new cloth patch. In both cases, the old skins and cloth are incompatible with the new, resulting in old wineskins cracking and wine spilling out and the old cloth ripping more when attached to the new cloth patch.

Without reading lots of commentary I latched on to an idea that our new creation in Christ doesn't fit well with our old sinful habits and self-dependent behaviors. Trying to keep one foot in the past and the other in the present reality of peace and joy through "Trust, Obey, Listen and Rejoice" is incompatible. Sooner or later, the new will give way to the old, and new life in Christ will deteriorate. You could say the waters of salvation will pour out of the old corrupt skins of sin and rebellion.

Lord, I am reminded daily that my new life in You is tender and subject to the devil's lies and deceit. I feel like the enemy expects me to fall eventually, so I must recommit my life and my heart to You each day. Through Your grace and assurance of everlasting life I am bolstered and can continue my journey down the path You have laid out for me. Seek first the kingdom of God and all His righteousness, and everything I need will be added.

On the Road to Emmaus—"Didn't Our Hearts Burn Within Us?"

At the time immediately following Christ's resurrection, His disciples were trying to process all that had happened and were missing badly their friend and Lord. Jesus gradually revealed Himself to them, beginning with Mary Magdalene, and, as written in the Gospel of Luke, He came alongside a couple of His followers walking to Emmaus. Jesus disguised His identity and engaged the two in a conversation about His recent crucifixion and death. These followers had not yet come to understand Christ as having redeemed them from their sins and enabled everlasting life in heaven. Instead, they were lamenting, having hoped Jesus would have been their Messiah.

With His true identity hidden, Jesus redirected His followers, explaining the prophets had written that the Messiah would have to suffer and He was, in fact, Jesus. Only when He broke bread with His followers that evening did Jesus permit them to see Him, this fellow traveler, as their Lord. As quickly as this revelation occurred, Jesus disappeared from sight. Amazed at what they had just witnessed, the followers then remarked: "Didn't our hearts burn within us as He talked with us on the road and explained the Scriptures to us?" (Luke 24: 32).

The significance of having a "burning heart" differentiates a believer who professes Christ as Lord and Savior from another believer whose life is transformed because of a faith and trust that nothing else is needed, except the love of Jesus. This divine love reduces much of what the world deems as important to clutter and sparks in us a desire to seek only the wisdom and courage to know God's will and then manifest His purpose for us in our lives. There will be times of celebration as well as times of suffering and disappointments; yet peace and joy will reign as we rest assured that God's infinite love will sustain us and His promise of everlasting life supersedes all else.

The journey to having a burning heart for Jesus requires a gradual emptying of our worldly cares and concerns. Sure, we have our responsibilities to our families, our neighbors and our community. Consider all else that consumes our time, emotions and energy, including pursuit of things, ambitions, worrying over promotions or loss of status or not being appreciated by our colleagues. There are sinful tendencies, such as speaking unkindly about our neighbor behind his back, having lustful thoughts about our neighbor's spouse or striving to "one up" our neighbor with clothes and cars and just thinking we're more important.

The journey to unloading all our worldly baggage begins with this daily affirmation from Scripture: "But seek first His kingdom and His righteousness, and all these things (all that you need) will be given to you as well" (Matthew 6:33). Pray each day that God will send the Holy Spirit to guide you, away from the inadequacy of self-reliance, toward becoming more reliant on God. He will set a path for you to follow, supplying all the provisions needed to sustain you. As a transformed believer, you may be more apt to witness to your neighbor of your faith and trust in God and thereby lifting up, not putting down, your neighbor.

Father, give me the fortitude to seek more of You and less of me and my meaningless distractions. Give me grace to quit waiting on others to affirm my value as a person and focus instead on Your Son, Jesus, through whom all value and worth are derived. Fill the void left by my pride and sense of esteem with the love of Jesus, which satisfies all our hungers and brings calm, peace and joy. May my heart too begin to burn for You as the only sustainable source of life everlasting.

We adore You, O Christ, and we praise You! By Your cross, death and resurrection You have redeemed the world!

Emboldened by the Love of Jesus

On this Pentecost Sunday we recall the arrival of the paraclete or advocate as promised by Jesus. On this day the Holy Spirit descended upon the twelve apostles, energizing the church of Jesus Christ. (see Acts 2: 1-13) The directive Jesus gave to go and make disciples of all nations, baptizing them in the name of the Father and of the Son and of the Holy Spirit, is the living legacy which we as Christians must embrace on a personal level (Matthew 28:19).

Pentecost represents an opportunity in the present to become emboldened by the love of Jesus and share this love with others. We are called to push ourselves beyond our comfort zones. There must be someone in our lives in distress, needing a phone call or personal visit. If not, arrange to visit a nursing home where your presence and a kind word can light up the day for those who rarely have visitors. How about planning to pray on the sidewalk outside an abortion clinic or volunteering to work on behalf of the poor?

We recall Jesus saying, "I was hungry and you gave me something to eat, I was thirsty and you gave me something to drink, I was a stranger and you invited me in, I needed clothes and you clothed me, I was sick and you looked after me, I was in prison and you came to visit me." We must see the face of Christ in all people, despite their circumstances or brokenness, as we were told: "Whatever you did for one of the least of my brothers and sisters of mine, you did for me" (see Matthew 25:35-40).

Notes from a Carmelite Retreat at St. Bernard's Abbey in Cullman, Alabama

> "Today, if you would hear His voice, Do not harden your hearts" (Psalm 95: 7-8).

Here are some thoughts about a weekend retreat I just attended with the Lay Carmelite Community, of which I am a member and in my first year of formation. There's much to know about Carmelites, their history, St. Teresa of Avila, St. Therese of Lisieux, and the other super saints, as well as the Carmelite charism of contemplation, nurtured through a life of prayer, community and service. For me, the call to Carmel stemmed from a personal desire to experience God in a deeper, more profound way so I might more clearly understand His will and purpose in my life.

A personal highlight of our time at St. Bernard's Abbey, a Benedictine monastery and retreat center, was an impromptu get together on Saturday with the only three men of our community, including me, to study the history of the Carmelites. We met at what seemed to be an unusual setting, the Abbey's cemetery chapel, close to the resting place of the many monks who had served at St. Bernard's over the past 125 years.

The particular lesson we discussed had to do with the role of the prophet Elijah, and Our Lady, in Carmelite history. Elijah harkened back to the time of the Desert Fathers, who experienced God's presence despite the harsh, austere desert conditions and founded the first Carmelite community at Mt. Carmel, located in Israel, overlooking the Mediterranean Sea. Our Lady has been considered a guiding light of Carmel, as the "Star of the Sea," or Stella Maris. As we discovered, the Holy Spirit may show up in unusual places, including cemetery chapels. As we were discussing the role of the Blessed Virgin, we became more keenly aware of a stained-glass window above the altar in the chapel, inscribed with the words Jesus spoke to the apostle John at Calvary: "Behold, your mother" (John 19:27). In addition, there was a large statue, situated above the altar, showing the suffering Mary holding her Son, Jesus, at the foot of the cross. This image was very much like the *Pieta*, with the anguish of a mother having lost her son quite evident on the face of Our Lady.

An insight soon flashed through me and my friends that we were in the very presence, in statue, block and glass, of what we were discussing concerning Our Lady. We were also reminded that Mary had suffered the pain of witnessing her Son's crucifixion and death. We could in some manner relate to her sorrow, knowing the way to the true source of peace, joy and consolation is the Son of Man, who accepted death on the cross so we may have life and have it more abundantly!

"The More Human He Was, the More Divine He Was"

> "While everyone was marveling at all that Jesus did, he said to His disciples, 'Listen carefully to what I am about to tell you: The Son of Man is going to be delivered into the hands of man'" (Luke 9: 43-45).

It's our humanness, with all our joys, struggles, setbacks and elation, that compels us as Christians to draw closer to Christ, our only reliable source of connection and comfort, placing all in the context of the salvation message. But for the Son of Man all would be lost, with no way to reconcile the disappointment of our human frailties with the deep-seated need to be purified and made whole in the eyes of our Savior.

Just as the Son of Man suffered terrible indignities at the hands of His human tormentors, culminating in death on the cross, we too must be slain to the flesh, even if tormented by the world in which we live. In dying to ourselves, our carnal nature and our own misguided hopes in being satisfied by what the world can deliver, we can join our sufferings with those of Jesus at Calvary and thereby stand to inherit the legacy of eternal life, joined with God in heaven.

The quote "The more human He was, the more divine He was" is attributed to Pope Leo the Great. Living in the fullness of the human experience, Jesus experienced the same range of emotions, the same joys and heartbreaks, which had to add much poignancy to His divine nature. His love for us had to be made perfect through walking in our shoes, making His calling to give His life for us more compelling and heartfelt. He died for us not just because we needed redemption; rather His deep empathy and love for us demanded it.

By Jesus becoming the Son of Man, He became the instrumentality of the Father to give us hope, to cleanse us from our sin debt and to provide those of us who believe in Him an unconditional fatherly embrace. It was not in spite of our sins, but because of the tender heart of the Father and the Son of Man, that we were saved.

Advent—A Time for Spiritual Regeneration

"He who was seated on the throne said, 'I am making everything new!'" (Revelation 21:5).

As we begin the season of Advent we have yet another opportunity to take stock of our lives, to reexamine the integrity of our walk with Christ. Are we making God's will and purpose the centerpiece of our daily activities? Is love of God and love of neighbor at the core of our thoughts and actions, or have we become a bit lukewarm, finding things and worldly pursuits capturing more of our attention than the saving of our souls?

Preparing for the birth of Jesus is of course more than the starting of a new liturgical calendar or the kick-off of holiday festivities. Jesus came for one reason, to overcome Satan and death, to make possible life everlasting in heaven. This Christian birthright is always available to those who believe, knowing that Christ, through His death and resurrection, gives us a second chance to renounce our sins, to ask for forgiveness, securing our place in heaven, thereby bringing us a healthy measure of peace and joy in this life.

Regeneration is synonymous with being born again. I have heard a popular evangelist, at the end of each broadcast, ask his congregation to recite a short prayer that by confessing your sins and making Jesus the Lord of your life you are born again. Perhaps that's all it takes for some Christians; but in my own experience walking that straight and narrow path requires lots of grace, divine forgiveness, daily reconciliation of my thoughts and actions, and taking time for spiritual regeneration. The harder I work at getting and keeping things right with Christ, the more difficult it becomes to stay in rebellion with my Savior. Over time, my default position moves more to Jesus and less to the ways of the world. That said, Satan is always close by, ready to trip me up, as if to knock me off my spiritual pedestal should I begin to think it is all about me and not God.

So, if our spiritual default swings in the wrong direction, here's an opportunity for some introspection and recommitting to Christ. Let Advent be a time of renewal to daily prayer, to self-denial, to considering the needs of others as foremost during this season of giving. Consider the apostle Paul's divinely inspired words in 2 Corinthians 5:17: "Therefore, if anyone is in Christ, the new creation has come: The old has gone, the new is here!"

"Lord, You Seduced Me, and I Was Seduced"

This actually comes from the Old Testament, the book of Jeremiah. (See Jeremiah 20:7) (JUB). It's hard to equate being drawn to God as a type of seduction, which seems more like the act of a sinful man than of God seeking our souls. I actually like the description, which I saw on the video about the Carthusian monks in France, whose lives are centered around silence and prayer toward finding a deeper connection with Christ.

God is not sitting back waiting for us to come to know His goodness and glory. He desires our souls for His kingdom, despite our lack of interest. He seeks ways to show His love for us, trying to bring us respite from the frustrations of our self-dependency. He pursues us.

All God wants is for us to say, "Yes, Lord." Through Jesus, everlasting life has been secured through forgiveness and redemption for our sins. The Holy Spirit is always there to guide us and direct our paths. As a child of God, I feel special that God longs for my love, my devotion, giving all I have to serve Him.

Lord, today I say yes to Your call to seek first the kingdom of God and Your righteousness, knowing all else will be provided. May I "seduce" others for the salvation of their souls through You and only You. Let my Christian example of love compel my neighbor to find true comfort, peace and joy, following "Trust, Obey, Listen and Rejoice"as a pathway.

Jesus, talk to me, talk to my spirit;
Jesus, speak to me, speak to my heart!

"I Am the Bread of Life"

"I am the living bread that came down from heaven. Whoever eats this bread will live forever. This bread is my flesh, which I will give for the life of the world" (John 6:51).

"Very truly I tell you, unless you eat the flesh of the Son of Man and drink his blood, you have no life in you" (John 6:53).

The miracle and wonder of God the Father giving His only Son to atone for our sins, and then having the body and blood of Jesus serve as spiritual food for our life journey, is mystical yet profoundly important to being a Christian. I am sure the apostles were puzzled, if not frightened, when Jesus spoke about eating His flesh and drinking His blood as necessary to securing an abundant life in this world and everlasting life in heaven.

The Jews were accustomed to the Old Testament stories about God the Father providing manna in the desert and meeting other temporal needs. In the lifetime of Jesus there was an expectancy that the Messiah would do the same, lifting up His people, providing them security, safety and prominence as their leader and king. As we know, Jesus certainly did not fit that profile, and His counter-cultural pronouncements about turning the other cheek and saying the first shall be last and so on were hard for them to fathom. The presence of Jesus and His revolutionary messages posed a threat to the establishment and set the stage for confrontation and ultimately Calvary.

"Bread of life" became the embodiment of the New Covenant through Jesus, who freed us from our sin debt through His death and resurrection and provided manna that would not decay. God the Father, having been a divine source of help and inspiration in the Old Testament, became a living presence and source of strength within us through Jesus, in the New Testament.

While Christians may view the mandate from Jesus that we must eat His flesh and drink His blood as only a call to emulate Christ in our thoughts, words and actions, we as Catholics take a more literal view. In Catholicism the Holy Eucharist is a centerpiece of the sacrifice of the Mass, a sacrament, the substantive presence of Jesus, body, blood, soul and divinity, which is received through the consecrated bread and wine.

This "real presence" recalls the breaking of the bread at the Last Supper and Jesus through the action of His breaking bread with His two fellow travelers after their journey to Emmaus. By receiving the Holy Eucharist, Catholics see not a symbol, but the substance of Jesus, as spiritual food promised by Christ.

The bread of life, contained in the sacrifice of His body and blood at Calvary, then recalled and renewed through the celebration of the Eucharist, has been Jesus' legacy and gift to us, giving us strength and staying power, ensuring us true peace and joy!

Jesus, the bread of life, who takes away the sins of the world, have mercy on us!

Jesus, the bread of life, who takes away the sins of the world, sustain us with Your infinite love and peace!

How God Reveals Himself to Us

"'But what about you,' He (Jesus) asked, 'Who do you say that I am?' Simon Peter answered, 'You are the Messiah, the Son of the living God.' Jesus replied, 'Blessed are you, Simon, son of Jonah, for this was not revealed to you by flesh and blood, but by my Father in heaven'" (Matthew 16:15-17).

"I want you to know, brothers and sisters, that the gospel I (Paul) preached is not of human origin. I did not receive it from any man, nor was I taught it; rather I received it by revelation from Jesus Christ" (Galatians 1:11-12).

Have you ever had an idea just pop into your mind on your way to work or in the shower or maybe during quiet prayer? This newfound insight or brainstorm might involve your family, your spouse or some nagging issue at work. The great idea may seem trivial or profound. Perhaps God might reveal an answer to life's questions, big or small, through the imposition of thoughts mixed with emotions, what some might call private revelations. I believe this is one of several ways that God makes His presence known to us.

In the Old Testament God made Himself known in very direct ways. Moses encountered God and received direction through the burning bush, compelling him to go back to Egypt and Pharaoh to demand freedom for the Israelites (see Exodus 3:1-15). Even in the New Testament Jesus struck Saul to the ground on his way to Damascus, chastising him for persecuting Christians and setting in motion an amazing transformation in him. Saul, whose name was changed to Paul, was destined to become one of the greatest missionary preachers for Jesus.

When we help someone less fortunate or take the time to listen and offer encouragement, we encounter Jesus, offering solace and relief to our neighbor, as if to somehow relieve Him of some of the pain He suffered on our behalf. The good example of our neighbor or a powerful sermon may inspire us to virtue, with God speaking to us and revealing His plan through another person.

Of course, reading Scripture allows us to see God through divine revelations to the Old Testament prophets and New Testament evangelists. One of my favorite readings from the Gospel of Matthew (6:33), where Jesus instructed us to seek first God's kingdom and His righteousness, knowing all else we need will be added, has been particularly helpful to me in setting priorities and relying on God's love to see me through all seasons of life.

Living my faith as a Catholic Christian brings me to a closer walk with Jesus, particularly through the Mass and the Sacrament of the Holy Eucharist. I believe I receive the body, blood, soul and divinity of Jesus through holy communion, the Eucharist, which adds spiritual nourishment and strength to face and overcome the trials of the day. My Catholic faith community provides personal support, while I experience Jesus in a special way through the ministries and outreach of His church.

Those who have chosen a contemplative life, with long periods of silence and spiritual reflection, remove much of the external and internal noises that most of us deal with daily. Through the inner calming of the senses, the monastics say they are able to commune more deeply with God in prayer, experiencing great peace and joy through His warm embrace.

Father, You speak to our minds and hearts in so many ways. Send Your Holy Spirit so we may be better tuned in to hear Your voice and discern Your will. I realize that revelation may come dramatically or even as a whisper or a gentle touch that moves our hearts to action. I seek grace to emulate the example of Your Son and my Savior, Jesus, who denied Himself out of infinite love, carrying His cross to save us from sin. May I deny myself and renounce anything that separates me from fulfilling Your will and purpose for me, through the name of Jesus, I pray, amen.

The Mechanics of Emotion

> "Whoever wants to be my disciple must deny themselves and take up their cross and follow me" (Mark 8:34).

Advancing the art of marketing and advertising by drawing on human emotions to make the sale is not a new concept. That said, I believe the folks at Alpha Romeo have taken the zeitgeist of marketing to an even higher level with their 2017 commercials promoting an $80,000 sports sedan. In their promotional piece the red Alpha Romeo Guilia ("Julia") Quadrifoglio speeds around the mountainous Italian countryside while a seductive-sounding female narrator speaks of her longing for "the perfect escape from monotony," preferring "power over passive" and "elusive over usual" while leaving the boring and predictable car (or man?) behind.

While this is only about buying a new car, Alpha Romeo is attempting to leverage human emotions in a big way. They call it *"La meccanica delle emozioni,"* or "The Mechanics of Emotion." The idea is that merging the aspirations of the human heart with the art, design and performance of the driving machine can create the ultimate car ownership experience. On a more practical level, this is all about enticing potential buyers to check out the new Alpha Romeo, intimating that one's standing as a full sensory, enlightened man or woman, who is anything but boring, passive or monotonous, will be enhanced.

After plopping down $80 K plus, the elated buyer may have forgotten to check out some of the automobile reviews on the Guilia Quadrifolgio and find this masterpiece of Italian engineering has some flaws. For a moment or two, the buyer might have the rush of feeling powerful and more interesting, but in due course the sexy female narrator will be forgotten and the reality of big car payments and nagging thoughts of "what was I thinking?" will take her place.

As a car guy, I once lived a bit vicariously through my auto purchases and was never satisfied for long before wanting to look at newer models. That's the way it goes with cars and with most anything the world offers that sort of promises lasting happiness. It's no wonder so many people suffer from depression and disillusionment, trying to satisfy their longings mostly with things and worldly relationships, only to be disappointed and wanting even more.

As the Son of Man, Jesus Christ epitomized "the perfect escape from monotony" and "elusive over usual." His pronouncements were so counter-cultural for His times, including the "last shall be first, and the first shall be last"(see Matthew 20:16); "if someone slaps you, turn the other cheek" (see Matthew 5:39); and "it's not what comes into your mouth that defiles you, but what comes out of your mouth." (see Matthew 15:11). The salvation message required not more of the world, but relying solely on the the love of Jesus to sustain us and rescue us from our preoccupation with stuff.

How's that as an alternative to "boring and predictable"? After all, Jesus promised, "I have come that they may have life, and have it more abundantly" " (John 10:10). (NKJV)

Let's change the Alfa Romeo commercial to instead placing Jesus Christ as the perfect foil to the allure of exotic automobiles, requiring little out-of-pocket costs other than giving of ourselves in service to God and neighbor and practicing greater self-discipline and simplicity. Let's place Jesus as the perfect path toward breaking free from the bondages of unhealthy attractions and sinful proclivities. Let's place Jesus as the only hope of redemption and life everlasting in heaven, thus the only true and lasting source of peace and joy.

Feel better? I do already as I wave good-bye to the notions of owning a red, $80,000 Alpha Romeo.

"Jesus, meek and humble of heart, make my heart like unto Thine!" (A prayer to obtain humility by St. Therese of Lisieux)

"He Must Become Greater; I Must Become Less"

From the Gospel of John, we read how the ministries of John the Baptist and Jesus of Nazareth were active around the same time, and there was some confusion as to the importance of each. In response, John the Baptist was quick to set the record straight that he was not the Christ, but the one who would present Christ to us. Understanding his mission clearly, John the Baptist declared that "He must become greater; I must become less," to avoid any confusion between his role as precursor and that of Jesus Christ, the true Messiah. (See John 3:30)

In our daily walk with Jesus, we face many challenges, becoming more aware of our own inadequacies and requiring a total dependence on God's mercy and grace to fulfill His purposes for us in this world. It takes time, prayer and daily renewal to seek first the kingdom of God and all His righteousness, in order to place the will of God in first position to our own ambitions and desires.

Allowing God's will and purposes to supersede all else brings a freedom from excessive fretting over our health, our families, our jobs, as God will provide all that we need to be faithful to

Him. Practicing faithfulness will bring about a lasting peace and joy, knowing that God's love for us is pervasive and everlasting.

Like John the Baptist, becoming less concerned about our own wishes and worldly pursuits and yielding more to the will of God in every aspect of our lives will pave the way for a greater supremacy of God in our lives. Pursuing this path opens the door to God working with us and through us to achieve some amazing things, even beyond the grasp of our imaginations! So this isn't about living a dull life to obtain everlasting life with God. By allowing more of God, we open ourselves to extraordinary possibilities and happiness, allowing a little of heaven on earth.

Lord, this is hard stuff, as the world throws me lots of mixed messages about pursuing happiness. Send Your Holy Spirit to help me discern what is Your will amid the background noise of daily life. By allowing more of You to become my priority, may You unlock Your blessings so I might do extraordinary things for You and Your kingdom, proclaiming Your message of love, redemption and salvation to my neighbors. I know lasting peace and joy will follow.

Jesus, talk to me, talk to my spirit;
Jesus, speak to me, speak to my heart!

Chapter 4

REJOICE

"You Can't Believe the Joy!"

Several years ago, I heard a Holy Week homily that related the story of a young seminarian (let's call him Peter) who had many fine qualities and a promising future as a Catholic priest. Unfortunately, Peter was stricken with cancer. His closest friends watched helplessly as he battled his disease, while amazed at his unrelenting trust, flowing from his love for Jesus, that everything would be okay.

Sad to say, the disease proved to be fatal, and before long, Peter became so weak that he was unable to get out of his bed and could only speak in a whisper. Right before he died, Peter motioned to one of his friends to come closer to his bed so he could convey a message. As the friend drew close, Peter whispered to him, "You can't believe the joy!" Peter repeated the same words and soon passed away.

I don't intend to depress you with this story but to give hope that in all our many struggles and pains, we can rely on the peace and joy that flows from a Christ-centered life. Our joy, flowing from our redemption and Christ's promise of eternal life, will transcend suffering and disappointment.

Father, help me find comfort in Your divine Son, and through Your grace give me the confidence to keep my gaze on You to see me through the darkest days. Let not my adversities rob me of my positivity. May I too have enough faith and confidence to keep my joy, even in the worst of circumstances.

"Be Anxious for Nothing"

> "Be anxious for nothing, but in everything by prayer and supplication, with thanksgiving, let your requests be made known to God; and the peace of Christ, which surpasses all understanding, will guard your hearts and minds through Jesus Christ" (Philippians 4:6-8) (NKJV)

Years ago I first heard that maintaining a consistent exercise regimen would help relieve anxiety and depression. I believe there is something to that, with our bodies releasing endorphins, with the potential for relieving pain and producing positive feelings. This idea actually got me exercising regularly.

In our increasingly secularized, stressed-out culture, people have come to rely more and more on readily available prescription drugs to elevate their moods or suppress their emotions. When going it alone, saying, "It's all up to me to make this work," emotional exhaustion may not be far away. Turning to these psychotropic wonder drugs, a self-sufficient society can at least feel artificially confident and happy.

As committed Christians, we should know that a better and more reliable source for relieving emotional stress is a daily regimen of prayer and spiritual reflection. Setting our sights on doing God's will and serving His purpose for us in our lives is a good start. Examining our consciences each day, regularly confessing our sins and gradually amending our behavior in a manner that is pleasing to God moves us down the path toward greater emotional equilibrium. Last, unconditionally surrendering our ambitions, our sense of control and our agendas, depending instead on the infinite love of God to guide our thoughts and actions, will gradually bring us to a more sustainable peace and joy, believing God allows all things to happen for the good of our souls.

At the core of developing a steady and calming reliance on God is acquiring a deep and abiding faith, which takes time to nurture. Remember that the apostles, having witnessed amazing healings and other miracles performed by Jesus, nonetheless became frightened during a storm on the Sea of Galilee. Even though Jesus accompanied them in the boat, their faith was not yet strong enough to know Jesus would see them through the storm (Mark 4:35-41).

Knowing we too will face uncertainties and may become gripped with fear, we have to develop a stronger trust that God will see us through the storm. When the dark clouds eventually dissipate and the light of God breaks through, our faith informs us that we will be just fine, although things may not always turn out the way we want. Let us learn to pray, "Lord, do with me as You will."

Heavenly Father, we praise You for the gift of our lives and the vast potential that exists therein for Your kingdom. Send Your Holy Spirit to give us discernment so we can know and actualize Your will and mission for us. By sending Your Son, Jesus, to conquer death, to redeem us from our sin and make possible life everlasting in heaven, we have hope and confidence that we too can overcome the forces of evil and find comfort in Your infinite love for us. By surrendering our hopes, ambitions, frustrations and potential to you, may this blunt our anxieties, knowing that lasting peace and joy are within our grasp. Amen.

Living in the Moment—Learning to Lighten Up in the New Year

"This is the day the Lord has made; let us rejoice and be glad in it" (Psalm 118:24). (ESV)

"Take my yoke upon you and learn from me, for I am gentle and humble in heart, and you will find rest for your souls. For my yoke is easy, and my burden is light" (Matthew 11:29-30).

"The Lord is my shepherd, I lack nothing. He
makes me lie down in green pastures; he leads
me beside quiet waters; he refreshes my soul"
(Psalm 23:1-3).

I watched some of this morning's edition of "Meet the Press"
and found myself getting all worked up about the constant
banter over the election and seemingly endless investiga-
tions about the Russians and the FBI and so forth. I finally had
enough, turned off the set and took a long walk on an unsea-
sonably warm, shiny January day. Now enjoying the day, more
worries come at me about everything from work to home to
finances—you know, the usual.

God created us with the capacity to complicate our lives.
Yet He sent His Son to simplify things, atoning for our sins and
opening the door to everlasting life in heaven. The Son of Man
gave us instructions on decompressing our emotions, with
words such as "My yoke is easy, my burden is light" (Matthew
11:29-30) and "Unless you change and become like little children, you will never enter the kingdom of heaven" (Matthew
18:2-4). That child-like faith, believing without question that
all is just fine, oblivious to anything but the love of the Father
to sustain us, is the destination we should seek.

A while back, I heard the phrase "being present in the
moment" as an exhortation to be totally engaged, making the
most of each day, each hour and each encounter. Too often
we are so caught up in worries about the future or regrets
about our past that we cannot focus much on the beauty and

simplicity of the present. Distracted, we can easily forget to enjoy the warmth of the sun on our faces on a sunny day, the sweet fragrance of spring flowers blooming or the pleasure I once experienced watching my grandchildren captivated as they chased baby chickens. It's in these majestic yet common experiences we find the hand of a loving God.

We read in the Bible that our heavenly Father doesn't miss a beat, that a sparrow doesn't fall from the sky without His knowing it and even the hairs on our head are numbered (see Matthew 10:29-30). If we trust that God has our best interests at heart, then why fret so much, why become so anxious, why act as if it is up to each of us to solve our problems and otherwise fix everything that seems broken? Maybe we have relied little on our belief in God, instead relegating the practice of our faith mostly to Sunday worship or otherwise to be invoked when we're frightened or in some trouble.

Perhaps a little more focus on daily prayer and devotions, attending weekday Mass for us Catholics and interspersing thoughts of praise throughout the workday might restore some calm. Even if our feelings continue to bring our fears and uncertainties to the surface, give God praise anyway until feelings catch up to our knowing He has all under control.

When Jesus instructed us to become like little children to enter the kingdom of heaven, He was calling us to embrace a child-like faith, believing unconditionally that our Father would see to our needs (see Matthew 18:2-4). No matter what challenges we face, we should strive to have a wide-eyed, unbridled optimism that God loves us infinitely, and we can rest, knowing His grace is sufficient to conquer any adversary.

Father, teach me to find solace in knowing the gift of Your Son, Jesus, saved me from my sins and made possible life everlasting in heaven. This is reason enough to be confident and joyful. Yet the ways of the world and presence of evil wreak havoc on my emotions, tempting me to reject Your commandments, to live a rebellious life. I pray for grace to reject anything that pulls me away from Your love and the fortitude to confess my sins and amend my life, thereby bringing restoration to my soul.

May I be present in the moment, remembering to bask in the warmth of the morning sun, sensing the glow of Your love for me!

Adding Vibrancy to Our Christian Witness

"You are the salt of the earth. But if the salt loses its saltiness, how can it be made salty again? It is no longer good for anything, except to be thrown out and trampled underfoot" (Matthew 5:13).

"Taste and see that the Lord is good; blessed is the one who takes refuge in him" (Psalm 34:8).

While there is a sense of reverence and awesomeness as we consider the glory of God in our lives and in the world, this doesn't always translate into a passion and vibrancy in our daily walk with the Lord. Spreading the gospel message of redemption and salvation through the cross and resurrection of Christ is more than an intellectual exercise or exposition about our faith. Effective witnessing requires an authentic, friendly, heartfelt expression of our love of God and neighbor that wells up from our spirit. Our message should speak to our struggles, our victory over flesh and our unconditional dependence on the undeserved grace of Jesus, setting straight our crooked paths and making all things possible. Our words and deeds can give hope to those who are lost and desperate for a new life that calls out their best potential.

Last month I had two very fervent but friendly Jehovah's Witnesses come knocking on my door. As many have experienced, their prepared comments and pitch were solely based on their translation of the Bible, which was amplified in several tracts they brought with them and offered to me. These well-intentioned folks were certainly brave to knock on doors, doing cold canvassing for God; yet their message went no further than attempting to make an intellectual appeal to me to essentially see things their way. From my encounter there was no real effort to make an emotional appeal or speak to what positive impact their message might have on my life.

Contrast that approach with one taken by the senior pastor of Tabernacle Baptist Church in Augusta GA, Rev. Dr. Charles Goodman, who gave a Martin Luther King Day speech in

January at First Presbyterian Church in Augusta, which can be found on YouTube. Goodman brings the gospel to life in a vivid and vibrant manner. Calling out the realities of our brokenness and that of the world, Goodman invokes the mercy and infinite love of our Savior, as a mighty force that offers hope, conquers our worries and gives us confidence that God will prevail in our lives. While we may have significant theological differences as Christians, I can't deny that Goodman's approach is powerful and gets his church members up on their feet and pumped about their walk and witness.

The point here is that our faith and our walk must be aligned, coming from the heart, alive, passionate, and thus more likely to be infectious to all who hear our witness. Otherwise, we're left with convincing or being convinced about the better argument and who can better articulate their beliefs. Once the heart is ready, the hunger for the truth will compel a person to seek answers and perhaps, along the way, become more receptive to sincere personal apologetics about the message of hope, peace and joy in the life of a committed Christian.

Effective evangelization begins with reconciling our own inconsistencies between our words and actions, confessing our sins, believing God can make all things new again (see Revelation 21:5). Effective evangelization requires making emotional connections with people where they are and nudging them along, not by hard judgments, but by our own example of love and joy, knowing salvation is possible for all through the saving grace of Jesus Christ. Amen!

"Life without Prayer Is Like Sunday without Chicken"

> "Blessed are the meek, for they will inherit the
> earth. Blessed are the pure in heart, for they
> will see God" (Matthew 5:5, 8).

When beginning my journey as an aspiring Lay Carmelite, I was assigned to our local Lay Carmelite Community's formation director, Paul. This rather quiet but friendly fellow at first appeared to a bit uncomfortable in this director role. Thinking to myself that he must be new to this, I wondered how he could help me, a cradle Catholic who had attended seminary and knew much, so I thought, about my faith.

With uncertain expectations Paul met with me one Thursday evening a month to walk through various chapters in our formation guide. He alternated with me, reading page-by-page, word-by-word, at his direction plowing slowly through each chapter. I always had lots of questions, reading between the lines, looking for hidden meaning pointing to eternity. Paul, on the other hand, kept it all very simple, and he was always comfortable seeing the hand of a loving God in the lives of Carmelites through the centuries. For him, it was always about prayer—that prayer was an important charism of life in Carmel, and prayer was always the one thing he valued the most as a Lay Carmelite.

I later learned Paul had grown up on a farm in Minnesota and was the second oldest of nine children. He said he knew at an early age he had a calling to a closer walk with Jesus and spent years seeking the fruition of that calling. By trade, Paul was a piano tuner. He told me about his travels, going from town to town, from home to home. He once forgot his tools, he explained to me, and had to drive a long way back to the shop for his special tuning instruments before heading back out to a client.

I found Paul had more patience than most, having learned through struggles to take life in stride. If I was late to our Thursday night meetings, Paul always waited on me and was okay with rescheduling if needed. Like Jesus, Paul was ready to help me in my formation, although he never pressed me, never forced the issue. When I was ready, Paul was there to help me.

Back to the life of Paul—he found love in his middle years, and his beloved wife learned to share Paul's love of prayer, even reading the Divine Office on her own, just as he had done for many years. Again, prayer was the one thing, a constant in his life, as he said, "Life without prayer is like Sunday without chicken," harkening back to simpler times as a Midwestern farmer's son. Paul also revealed that his precious wife had suffered from serious health and mobility challenges, which was very tough for him to bear, as he compared his quiet suffering to that of Mary toward her Son, who endured so much pain. Like Mary, Paul quietly accepted the hurt while rarely letting on to me how this must have troubled his spirit.

Once more about prayer—for me, a habit of prayer had been one of my biggest challenges spiritually, and it took a while before I realized Paul was gifting me with his love of prayer. Each month as we started our formation meetings, when Paul lit a small votive candle, placed in a small cobalt-blue glass vessel (as a tribute to Our Lady), I was reminded of the Scripture verse "For where two or three gather in my name, there am I with them" (Matthew 18:20). With Paul, I sensed God's presence, helping change my heart of stone to a heart of flesh.

In closing, Paul took his final professions as a Third Order Lay Carmelite in 2001 and has found comfort ever since, knowing this is what God called him to do for His kingdom. By helping form aspiring Lay Carmelites, like me, Paul has become a disciple of Jesus, helping save souls through his gentle, unassuming way of reassuring us that Jesus loves us infinitely.

Can We Begin to Experience Heaven on Earth?

"Hey, is this heaven? No, it's Iowa." (quote from movie *Field of Dreams*).

"All people are called to ultimately be totally united with Christ in heaven...we wish to start heaven here on earth." (from YouTube video on the Dominican Sisters of St. Cecilia in Nashville, Tennessee).

Many of us remember the movie *Field of Dreams*, including the poignant moment when the character played by Kevin Costner meets the ghost of his deceased father, who is no longer worn down by the cares of the world, but young again with lots of curiosity. The father, John Kinsella, in response to the wonder of seeing Ray, his son, and meeting his family, asks Ray if he is in heaven. As we recall in this famous line, Ray responds, "No, this is Iowa."

While heaven is our eternal reward as Christians for trusting in Jesus as our Lord and Savior, for many the concept of heaven assumes that our life on earth will, almost by definition, fall short of expectations. Our dreams may not come true, so therefore we might conclude that we too will become worn down by the concerns and disappointments of life, finding true and lasting happiness only in the hereafter. When measuring fulfillment in this world based on financial success, recognition and leaving a worldly legacy, the metrics may very well fall short of the mark.

In John 10:10, Jesus said He came into this world "that they might have life, and have it more abundantly." Finding a more fulfilling life requires less pursuing of things and more loving God and serving our neighbor. It is through self-denial, acknowledging our nothingness without the love and mercy of Jesus, that we begin to open our hearts to His plan and purpose. We thereby receive the grace necessary to manifest His mission for us on earth in pursuit of souls and furthering the needs of the kingdom of God. Yes, our goal is to be redeemed from our sins and live forever with Jesus in heaven, and it is possible to get an early start, experiencing a taste of heavenly bliss on earth.

The Catholic Dominican Sisters of St. Cecilia, in Nashville, Tennessee, have seen a vocation boom in recent years, as more and more young women are discerning vocations to the religious life. Their charism of being contemplative then sharing the fruits of their contemplation through their teaching ministry has placed them in schools around the world, including Aquinas College in Nashville, which they own and operate.

The Nashville Dominicans vow a life of total surrender to Christ, being willing to go wherever called and forsaking all things in reliance on the providence of God for all they need. Granted, this is radical stuff for most of us. Yet consider that their absolute submissiveness brings with it a sense of freedom, along with a happiness they can find nowhere else. In a world that promises so much but delivers very little that is of lasting value, it's no wonder that a life of denial and dependence solely on the love of God may be gaining in popularity.

So can we begin to experience heaven on earth? Having lasting peace and joy that is not dependent on anything the world can offer but rests completely on an abandonment to our ways, yielding to the will of God, may be the pathway to true holiness and sustainable happiness. When removing some of the burden and distraction of expectations the world places on our shoulders, we might open our eyes to the many gifts from God, including our children and grandchildren and the grandeur of nature. In desiring to have nothing but the love and mercy of Christ, our hearts are open to His direction, our spirits are calmed, and we too might ask, "Is this heaven?"

Receiving God's Mercy, the Greatest Act of Love

> "Then Peter came to Jesus and asked, 'Lord, how
> many times shall I forgive my brother or sister
> who sins against me? Up to seven times?' Jesus
> answered, 'I tell you, not seven times, but sev-
> enty-seven times'" (Matthew 18:21-22).

> "Straightening up, Jesus said to her, 'Woman,
> where are they? Did no one condemn you?'
> She said, 'No one, Lord.' And Jesus said, 'I do
> not condemn you either. Go. From now on, sin
> no more'" (John 8:10-11). (NASB)

In 2016, Pope Francis declared a year of mercy, signaling an
opportunity for all Christians to seek God's forgiveness and
extend mercy to all people, regardless of their circumstances
and despite their willingness to be open to the love of God.
Mercy is given freely by God and made perfect through the suffering, death and resurrection of His Son, Jesus. Our sin debt
has been paid one time, beginning with the sacrifice at Calvary,
and life in eternity with God is possible to all who believe and
seek forgiveness.

While I cannot exhaust the capacity of God to extend
pardon for my sins, I have learned that meaningful action to
change my behavior becomes critical to bringing my life into
a closer union with God. For me, receiving mercy is a call for
change to move away from thoughts, words and actions that

are contrary to the commandments and to embrace a life that is pleasing to God. I recall from my Catholic upbringing about "amending my life" upon receiving absolution through the Sacrament of Penance . In my Act of Contrition prayer, I spoke the words, "I detest all my sins because I dread the loss of heaven and the pains of hell."

So mercy is drawing from the endless reservoir of God's love, not so we can just feel good for the moment. Instead, this is about saving our souls from destruction and a life of separation from God in the hereafter. The stakes are very high, and to live another day in rebellion, without seeking God's forgiveness and striving to change our lives, is tantamount to living dangerously.

The other side of the mercy "coin" relates to extending compassion and forgiveness to our neighbor. I recall St. John Paul II, having recovered from a failed assassination attempt, going to visit his shooter in prison, offering forgiveness for the would-be assassin's despicable act. Just as Jesus died for our sins, without condition and despite our proclivity to offend Him, we must strive to offer mercy freely, even to those who offend or despise us and who may likely continue to do the same.

Here's a short prayer of thanksgiving: We adore You, O Christ, and we praise You. By Your holy cross, death and resurrection, You have redeemed the world! Our Christian faith is made perfect through our redemption. Everyone needs redemption, which to me means change.

Mercy is not about God being lovingly nonjudgmental or accepting of our poor choices as we double down on our sinful behavior. Mercy is about God forgiving us when we really deserve condemnation, enabling us to be saved and secure a place in heaven. For that to become real, we must take to heart the admonition that Jesus gave to the contrite woman caught in adultery. Jesus said, "I do not condemn you either. Go. From now on sin no more."

Jesus, talk to me, talk to my spirit;
Jesus, speak to me, speak to my heart!

Choosing to Be Happy

"**Happiness** is a mental or emotional state of well-being defined as positive or pleasant emotions ranging from contentment to complete joy" (Wikipedia).

"If a man has recently married, he must not be sent to war or have any other duty laid on him. For one year he is to be free to stay at home and bring **happiness** to the wife he has married" (Deuteronomy 24:5).

Several years ago, my wife Stephanie and I were walking through a hotel lobby on St. Simon's Island when we met two newlyweds who happened to be staying at this same hotel. The happy-looking couple was in their sixties, and they let us know about their children from previous marriages and remarked how they were so fortunate to find love later in life. As Stephanie was discussing bridal gowns with the elegant-looking lady, I asked the gentleman about how this had worked so well for him, to which he replied, "I choose to be happy."

My first impression to this choice of happiness was that the gentleman may not really be as excited about this marriage as he had initially let on. I thought to myself, "Shouldn't happiness sort of happen, given all the right things are in place and most especially that husband and wife love one another?" As I pondered all of this, I began to realize that being content is tied to emotions or feelings, which may not always match up to positive situations and circumstances. A new mother is likely ecstatic about her new baby yet later may experience postpartum depression. I have heard of Christians, even saintly souls like Mother Teresa, who led exemplary lives of service to God's kingdom but also endured periods of darkness and spiritual dryness, feeling distant for a brief time or for a long season, not sensing or feeling the warmth of God's love.

Popular culture adds even more confusion to the happiness experience. Not being debt free or lacking the latest electronic devices or the ideal body shape may depress the otherwise contented person into thinking, "What I have or what I am doing is just not good enough."

For Christians, tying our state of well-being to anything but the love and mercy of God is nothing short of a fool's errand. Sometimes we have to ask for the grace to suppress our emotions, instead choosing to be happy with what God has provided us, which always includes many blessings. Perhaps if we turn away from self-gratification to *more* serving our neighbor, that might bring us *more* lasting joy.

One of my favorite verses from the New Testament applies here. "But seek first the kingdom of God, and his righteousness; and all these things will be added unto you" (Matthew 6:33). While we can follow this direction, our emotions may not always agree and may compel us to take alternate, less "righteous" paths toward achieving the good feelings, getting that endorphin-rush of pleasure. Choosing to be happy means working to align our emotions with the path of righteousness, even during periods of darkness, trusting that the peace and joy of having God's will and purpose at the center of our lives will follow.

Do You Believe in Miracles?

Miracle: "An extraordinary event manifesting divine intervention in human affairs" (Merriam-Webster).

> "Another of his disciples, Andrew, Simon Peter's brother, spoke up, 'Here is a boy with five small barley loaves and two small fish, but how far will they go among so many?' Jesus said, 'Have the people sit down.' There was plenty of grass in that place, and they sat down (about five thousand men were there). Jesus then took the

loaves, gave thanks, and distributed to those who were seated as much as they wanted. He did the same with the fish" (John 6:8-11).

"Truly I tell you, if you have faith as small as a mustard seed, you can say to this mountain, 'Move from here to there,' and it will move. Nothing will be impossible for you" (Matthew 17:20).

My own miracle occurred through the love of Jesus, who in His wisdom, allowed me to be tested by Satan, to see if my devotion to Him was genuine and deep. In the midst of battle Jesus had provided me with a spiritual boost in the form of an older Roman Rite (Latin Mass) Catholic Church, St. Francis de Sales, in Mableton, Georgia. The chaplain at Cobb Hospital made me aware of this church, and this particular evening I happened to go looking, using my GPS, to find St. Francis.

A miracle of sorts occurred after I pulled up in the church parking lot, finding the lot empty, the church doors locked and not much going on. As I was walking back to my car to leave, a SUV pulled up, with an older looking gentleman stepping out and asking if he could help me. I felt a bit like a trespasser but introduced myself, and the gentleman and his wife quickly said hello and proceeded to tell me all about their church. They explained that there were about four hundred members and the church existed more as a destination parish than a local faith community, which I found interesting and intriguing.

The lady was there to practice on the church organ, and they invited me to look around. I began talking about growing up with the Latin Mass, and mentioning my time in the seminary, our large family and going on and on as I can do.

As I walked into the church, following the couple's lead by genuflecting, I quickly was taken in by the beauty, peace and majesty of the sanctuary. The altar and communion rail took me back more than fifty years, as the form of worship and liturgy goes back to the early 1960s, before Vatican II, when there seemed to be greater reverence and respect in the practice of Catholicism. In those years, clearer lines underscored what was truth and what was right or wrong. There was respect in the Catholic community for the role of the church and particularly around our liturgical celebrations, designed to inspire a call to holiness. That night all of my doubts and cares seemed to melt away as I knelt down for a few minutes and prayed.

If I wasn't sure about the hand of Jesus in my impromptu drive to St. Francis, I had no question when the parish priest showed up and said hello while I was in the sanctuary, that Jesus had just revealed Himself in a significant way to show me the next dimension in my journey toward a deeper walk with Him. The priest was dressed in a traditional, full black cassock and invited me to come to Mass and pray while I was visiting, which I did. He also suggested that I purchase a missal from the parish bookstore.

The next morning I arose with one thing on my mind, and that was to get to 6:30 morning Mass at St. Francis on time. I made it to the church a few minutes before Mass began. I watched the altar server genuflect as he moved from one side of the altar to the other, lighting just two candles for this Low Mass. When the Mass began, using the 1962 Latin missal as promulgated by St. Pope John XXIII, for a moment I was a spectator, not a participant, as I had long ago become accustomed to a more active role during the Mass, going back to the late 1960s. Today, Mass in most Catholic Churches is celebrated in the native tongue of the people, and is referred to as the Novus Ordo, or new order form of Mass, promulgated by Pope Paul VI. The Catholic Church refers to the celebration of the Latin Mass as the extraordinary rite.

Going to St. Francis Church helped awaken in me a sense of what God wants in my life, including keener attention to my faith, my family and my work. This means adhering to a more stringent set of principles around right and wrong behavior, knowing and abiding by truths that are infinite and immutable. Reading the 1962 Roman missal has taken me back to the pre-Vatican Council days, when my Catholic religious sisters (at Sacred Heart School in Augusta, Georgia), serving as my teachers and using the Baltimore Catechism, laid down the rules about righteous living. Everything taught about right and wrong fit tightly together, as there seemed to be less confusion, flowing from the more contemporary notions of morality being more situational or a matter of conscience. I have taken an additional step of purposely limiting exposure to television, music and internet use, allowing more quiet and calm, thereby devoting more time for reflection and permitting God to speak to me. Consequently, I am more enthusiastic about my future and how God might use me, through the written reflections, for helping save souls and taking His salvation message, one of peace and joy, to the world.

Father, thank You for the many blessings You have bestowed upon me, including the recent reintroduction to the Latin Mass. May I be an instrument for You, through my written and spoken words, so I might help others find hope and be saved through the example and heavenly wisdom shown by your very special Son, Jesus, amen.

Grace is Amazing!

Growing up as a Roman Catholic, I don't remember much said about divine grace but did remember sin had consequences, including purgatory and hell. Seemed like you were never completely "off the hook" for your past transgressions.

I have come to learn that grace is that extra something, like a spiritual B-12 shot, we receive from God. Grace is a super-enabler to living a good life. It is not earned or deserved but available from Christ as a type of divine impetus, a means of defeating the devil and all of his lies. Grace gives us hope that, through confession/reconciliation, Christ has boundless capacity to forgive *and* forget our sins. Grace helps us avoid temptations, resisting the opportunity to sin and providing greater self-awareness of pitfalls.

As a booster shot of Christ's love, grace also gives us a quiet confidence that we can face today's challenges, knowing Christ will put a path in front of us, where failure in His eyes is not possible, so long as we "Trust, Obey, Listen and Rejoice".

So once we confess our spiritual failings and ask for forgiveness we truly have a clean slate and are "off the hook" in God's eyes. Let's not allow yesterday's failings to dictate our positive potential today and tomorrow. Strive to live a good and holy life, and ask God today and each day for His amazing grace!

It's All about Saving Souls

In today's Gospel reading from Luke we hear about Zacchaeus, who was a senior tax collector and reviled by many, who really wanted to see Jesus as He walked through Jericho. As Jesus approached, Zacchaeus, being short in stature, but tall in enthusiasm and determination, decided to climb a Sycamore tree so he could see over the gathering crowd and catch a glimpse of Jesus.

Lucky for Zacchaeus, Jesus noticed him looking from the tree and called him to climb down because Jesus said He wanted to stay at his house that day. Zacchaeus was overjoyed and welcomed Jesus, while others witnessing this interaction were critical, complaining that Jesus was going to stay at a known sinner's house.

Zacchaeus would have none of the negativity, instead pledging to give half of what he owned to the poor and to repay others he may have cheated as a tax collector four times the amount. Jesus then remarked that salvation had come to

Zacchaeus's house and that the Son of Man had come to save what was lost.

Today I also heard the homilist in describing the Gospel story say that Jesus plucked Zacchaeus from the tree, like ripened fruit, to satisfy His appetite for souls. Lord, we too must be all about bringing souls to the knowledge of Your love, redemption and salvation. May we renew our own commitment to You and rid ourselves of unnecessary worldly distractions, so we may be a witness to Your light and harvest souls for Jesus. Amen!

Remember to Count Your Blessings

"You prepare a table before me in the presence of my enemies . You anoint my head with oil; my cup overflows" (Psalm 23:5).

"In everything I did, I showed you that by this kind of hard work we must help the weak, remembering the words the Lord Jesus Himself said: 'It is more blessed to give than to receive'" (Acts 20:35).

Definition of a *blessing in disguise*: "A misfortune that unexpectedly turns into good fortune" (*American Heritage Dictionary of Idioms*).

When taking stock of all the blessings we receive, most of us might think first about our faith and family, our health, our vocation or life's work and, of course, our financial security. As we know, blessings come in many ways, whether directly through God's beneficence or indirectly in the midst of hardships or through the act of serving others through our treasure, our talents or our time. Remember that the ultimate blessing of our salvation came through the suffering and death of Jesus.

The blessing of a hardship, flowing from some setback or calamity in our lives, might flow from the lessons we learn from the experience, although consider the reality that God allows all things to happen for the good of our souls. When we are discouraged or frightened about some unwelcome event or change, I believe God is actually using the "bump in the road" to draw us closer to Him so we can more richly experience His infinite love, comfort and direction and hence receive the real blessing.

Having lots of things, meaning worldly possessions, may appear to be a nice blessing. Yet the human tendency to want more, never having enough and having to maintain what we have, often becomes a burden. Learning to do with less, exercising self-discipline and unloading some of our stuff, perhaps for the benefit of others, might quell the wanting for more, bringing a little peace and becoming another blessing in disguise.

Through the act of accepting our crosses each day, denying ourselves and allowing the love of God and neighbor to take first position in our lives, we become more open to God's direction, will and purpose for us. Keeping our gaze on God, we are enabled to see blessings in plenty and want, in good times and struggles. Whether fearful or serene, we trust we will be just fine.

> "Test me in this, says the Lord Almighty, and see
> if I will not throw open the floodgates of heaven
> and pour out so much blessing that there will
> not be room enough to store it" (Malachi 3:10).

God's bounty for those who love Him and follow His commandments is vast and immeasurable. Whatever we need in fulfilling His will and mission for our lives will be provided, including the absence of wanting anything but to serve God.

Father, we reflect on the gift of Your Son, Jesus, whose obedience unto death, through His suffering, crucifixion, death and resurrection, made possible the priceless blessing of life everlasting. All that Jesus did for us can be summed up in one word: *love*. May Your unconditional love inform all that we do, including our words and actions, so we might advance Your message of forgiveness and salvation to all, and maybe help save a soul or two in the process, through Jesus' name, we pray. Alleluia! Alleluia!

BIBLIOGRAPHY

Catechism of the Catholic Church, 2nd ed. Washington, DC: United States Conference of Catholic Bishops, 2000

Glueckert, Leopold, O. Carm. *Desert Springs in the City: A Concise History of the Carmelites.* Darien, Illinois: Carmelite Media, 2012

CPSIA information can be obtained
at www.ICGtesting.com
Printed in the USA
LVHW03s0314310818
588768LV00001B/35/P

9 781545 638514